BLACK DEMONS

BLACK DEMONS

The Media's Depiction of the
African American Male Criminal Stereotype

Dennis Rome

Crime, Media, and Popular Culture

Frankie Y. Bailey and Steven Chermak, Series Editors

PRAEGER

Westport, Connecticut
London

Library of Congress Cataloging-in-Publication Data

Rome, Dennis
    Black demons : the media's depiction of the African American male criminal stereotype /
Dennis Rome.
        p. cm.—(Crime, media, and popular culture, ISSN 1549-196X)
    Includes bibliographical references (p.   ) and index.
    ISBN 0-275-97244-5 (alk. paper)
    1. African Americans in mass media.   2. Crime in mass media.   3. Mass media—
United States.   I. Title.   II. Series.
P94.5.A37R66   2004
302.23'089'96073—dc22   2004044387

British Library Cataloguing in Publication Data is available.

Library of Congress Catalog Card Number: 2004044387
ISBN: 0-275-97244-5
ISSN: 1549-196X

First published in 2004

Praeger Publishers, 88 Post Road West, Westport, CT 06881
An imprint of Greenwood Publishing Group, Inc.
www.praeger.com

Printed in the United States of America

The paper used in this book complies with the
Permanent Paper Standard issued by the National
Information Standards Organization (Z39.48-1984).

10 9 8 7 6 5 4 3 2 1

For My Students

Contents

Series Foreword

This volume marks the launching of an exciting new interdisciplinary series on Crime, Media, and Popular Culture from Praeger Publishers. Because of the pervasiveness of media in our lives and the salience of crime and criminal justice issues, we feel it is especially important to provide a home for scholars who are engaged in innovative and thoughtful research on important crime and mass media issues.

This series will focus on process issues such as the social construction of crime and moral panics; presentation issues such as the images of victims, offenders, and criminal justice figures in news and popular culture; and effects such as the influence of the media on criminal behavior and criminal justice administration.

With regard to this latter issue—effects of media and popular culture—as this preface was being written, the *Los Angeles Times* and other media outlets reported that two young half-brothers (ages 20 and 15) in Riverside, California, had confessed to strangling their mother and disposing of her body in a ravine. The story was attracting particular attention because the brothers told police they had gotten the idea of cutting off her head and hands to prevent identification from a recent episode of the award-winning HBO series, *The Sopranos*. As the *Los Angeles Times* noted, this again brought into the spotlight the debate about the influence of violent media such as *The Sopranos*, about New Jersey mobsters, on susceptible consumers.

In this series, scholars engaged in research on issues that examine the complex nature of our relationship with media. Peter Berger and Thomas Luckman coined the phrase the "social construction of reality" to describe the process by which we acquire knowledge about our environment. They and others have argued that reality is a mediated experience. We acquire what Emile Durkheim described as "social facts" through a several-pronged process of personal experience, interaction with others, academic education, and, yes, the mass media. With regard to crime and the criminal-justice system, many people acqure much of their information from the news and from entertainment media. The issue raised by the previously mentioned report and other anecdotal stories of "copycat" crime is how what we consume—read, watch, see, play, hear—affects us.

What we do know is that we experience this mediated reality as individuals. We are not all affected in the same way by our interactions with mass media. Each of us engages in interactions with mass media and popular culture that are shaped by factors such as our social environment, interests, needs, and opportunities for exposure. We do not come to the experience of mass media and popular culture as blank slates waiting to be written upon or voids waiting to be filled. It is the pervasiveness of mass media and popular culture, and the varied backgrounds (including differences in age, gender, race and ethnicity, religion, etc.), that we bring to our interactions with media that make this a particularly intriguing area of research.

Moreover, it is the role of mass media in creating the much-discussed "global village" of the twenty-first century that is also fertile ground for research. We exist not only in our communities, our cities, and states, but in a world that spreads beyond national boundaries. Technology has made us a part of an ongoing global discourse about issues not only of criminal justice but of social justice. Technology shows us events around the world "as they happen." It was technology that allowed Americans around the world to witness the collapse of the World Trade Center's twin towers on September 11, 2001. In the aftermath of this "crime against humanity," we have been witnesses to, and participants in, an ongoing discussion about the nature of terrorism and the appropriate response to such violence.

In this first volume in our new series, we have brought together scholars from a wide range of disciplines to examine the role of mass media in the social construction of reality in the wake of an event, such as September 11, that affected us all in profound ways. This volume is only the first in a series that we expect to be both timely and significant.

Frankie Y. Bailey and Steven Chermak,
Series Editors

Preface

The main idea for this book was developed, in part, several years ago when Susan Smith, a young white mother of Union, South Carolina, strapped her small children into the backseat of her car and drove the car into a lake. Before she confessed to this act, she told police and representatives of the media that her car had been carjacked by an African American male. She gave the police a description of a young African American male wearing a skull cap: the image of a criminal for most Americans. A small group of my undergraduate students and a few of my faculty colleagues and I would frequently gather informally to discuss current events and issues that pertained especially to the African American community. It was through these impromptu and informal gatherings that Black Demons was born. I would like to thank, from the bottom of my heart, these strikingly brilliant people who comprised these gatherings: Professors Fred McElroy, Gloria Gibson, and Coramae Mann; among my favorite undergraduate students were Pete Adams, Philmore Hutchins, and Christopher Bickel. Special thanks go to Rahsaan Bartet for his selection of icons used for the "conceptual entrapment of media" schema in chapter 3 and for his countless trips to the library to corroborate sources.[1] My good friends and mentors David Takeuchi, Carla Howery and Norma Nager deserve special thanks for the unconditional love and support they continue to give me. Special gratitude is due also to Wendy Beck for her reading of earlier versions of this manuscript, and thanks to my friend and colleague Steve Chermak for whom without his encouragement and support this manuscript would not have come to fruition.

My family has always supported my academic endeavors and, for this, my love for them is relentless—special thanks to my wife Natalia who has been a great companion, friend and beacon of light during cloudy and foggy days. I am what I am, in part, because of the exceptionally talented students I have been privileged to work with over the years. To them this book is dedicated.

Dennis M. Rome

Introduction

Portions of these grim messages were extended to black men's violence, especially that of the "violent" black, lower-class male. I was told that all black men were inherently aggressive and violent. They, like white men, could rape, plunder, assault, and murder our souls. Poor black men with Negroid features were particularly inclined to this behavior. I therefore acquired a deep-seated fear of the "savage" nature of black men who could not control their pent-up aggressiveness, hatred, and sexual urges. Believing them to be inherently criminal, my black female elders considered poor black men as the "other."[1]

Another consequence for black America is that this "monster" image created by the white popular culture has been taken over by some poor blacks. According to Stallworth (1994), young black men and women both continue to follow patterns of slavery times. They become the monsters. Many fulfill white America's image of them legitimately by becoming successful gangsta rappers; others fulfill this image illegitimately by becoming "baaad niggers." Rappers, therefore, reinforce the popular belief that as "baaad-ass niggers" young blacks can achieve fame, recognition, and a sense of being (somebody). If they lose, however, they face a long stay in our jails and prisons or even bodily injury and death.[2]

The present study contends that the negative stereotypes that many people have of African American men are created to a significant degree by the mass media.

The media seems fixated on a controversial thesis that arose especially in the 1970s with the emergence of *blaxploitation films*: that there is a "black pathology," a fundamental weakness in African American families that can be traced to their experiences as slaves.[3] The news media, for example, have taken the lead in equating young African American males with aggressiveness, lawlessness, and violence. Likewise, the entertainment media have eagerly taken their cue from the journalists, and these false images not only affect race relations but also create a self-fulfilling prophecy for African American youngsters, whose limits of achievement can be predetermined for them by suggestions in the media.

A common stereotype about African American men, addressed in this book, is that they engage in drug abuse in disproportionate numbers. Statistics from the United States Department of Health and Human services illustrate that although eight percent of African Americans have used cocaine, eleven percent of whites have used the same drug.[4] This is, however, not the impression one gets from watching the evening news or even an episode of the television program *COPS*. This is especially detrimental to African American youth, both male and female—they see a litany of people who have done things wrong. They seldom see African Americans, particularly males, who are achievers. It is a dangerous tendency for them to think the only way black men can achieve or earn enough is to be involved in the illegal economy. Other common negative stereotypes depicted in mass media include the black male as a criminal and drug addict—there is also a recurring portrayal of the African American male as intellectually inferior.[5]

Just as the legendary Frederick Douglass argued that the "myth of the black rapist" was created to legitimize lynchings, this book underscores that a criminal image of the black male is being consistently used today to perpetuate dominant society's continued fear and subjugation of African Americans.[6] In addition, I provide a historical analysis of African Americans to illustrate the origin and extent to which dominant society has used negative stereotypes to retain African Americans as second-class citizens. The criminal depictions, often provided by mass media and society's subsequent belief that most African American males are criminals, are good examples of the damaging effects of negative stereotypes. In fact, in a survey conducted in 2000, whites were asked to evaluate on a scale of one to seven how violence prone blacks were; forty-seven percent chose the violent end (ranks 1–3) of the spectrum. When asked the same question about whites, only twenty-one percent placed whites as a group in the same ranks.[7]

In addition to very overt surveys like the one mentioned above, it is important to note that much of today's bias is covert and, in fact, covert bias is emerging as an important clue to the disparity between public opinion, as expressed by America's creed and social goals, and the amount of discrimination that still exists. Despite over thirty years of equal-rights legislation, the levels of poverty, education, and success vary widely across races. Discrimination continues in housing and real estate sales, and racial profiling is a common practice, even among ordinary citizens. Members of minorities continue to report humiliating treatment by store clerks, coworkers, and police. Although an African American man may dine in a fine restaurant anywhere in America, it can be embarrassing for him to attempt to flag down a taxi after that dinner.

A person who carries the stigma of group membership must be prepared for its debilitating effects. Studies indicate that African American teenagers are aware that they are stigmatized as being intellectually inferior and that they go to school bearing what psychologist Claude Steele has called a "burden of suspicion." Such a burden can affect their attitudes and achievement. Similarly, studies found that when college women are reminded that their group is considered bad at math, their performance may fulfill this prophecy.[8]

These shadows hang over stigmatized people no matter their status or accomplishments. They must remain on guard and bear an additional burden that may affect their self-confidence, performance, and aspirations. These stigmas have the potential to rob them of their individuality and debilitate their attempts to break out of stereotypical roles.

THE SOCIAL CONSTRUCTION OF CRIME

The theoretical underpinnings of the present study are implicit in its title and subtitle, namely, that our definition of crime is socially constructed mainly by mass media and, after further analysis, we find that crime is often associated with African Americans. The theoretical perspective known as the social construction of reality first introduced by Peter Berger and Thomas Luckmann and integrated into criminology by Richard Quinney better illustrate the impact of a pervasive mass media.[9] Under this theoretical view, people create reality and the world they believe exists is based on their individual knowledge and from knowledge gained from social interactions with other people. People then act in accordance with their constructed view of reality. There is a cyclical effect in constructing reality in that once people perceive concepts to be real, they go out and look for examples of these concepts. Katheryn Russell gives a good example of this conceptualization process in her pivotal book, *The Color of Crime: Racial Hoaxes, White Fear, Black Protectionism, Police Harassment and Other Macroaggressions*, in which she describes a short film she had seen entitled *The Slowest Car in Town*.[10] This film tells the story of a young black man, dressed in a business suit and carrying a briefcase, who enters an elevator on the eighteenth floor of an office building. The elevator makes four stops before reaching the lobby. With each stop someone white enters the elevator. Each white passenger sees something different. At the first stop, a white woman gets on the elevator and on discovering the race and sex of her fellow passenger, she makes a quick exit. Two white people get on at the next stop. They look at the black man and "see" an African bushman holding a spear and "hear" roaring African drum beats. The next whites who board the elevator envision the black man as a shackled convict, wearing prison stripes. Other passengers visualize him as a drooling crack addict who looks like a homeless beggar. By the time the elevator reaches the lobby, the black businessman no longer exists—he has been reduced to the image projected onto him by the white passengers.

According to Russell, what happened to the African American businessman on the elevator is termed "entrapment by media imagery."[11] Blacks are the repository for the American fear of crime. Ask anyone, of any race, to picture a criminal, and the image will have a black face. The link between blackness and criminality is routinized by terms such as "black-on-black crime" and "black crime."[12]

Moreover, research by a Pennsylvania State University (hereafter, Penn State) media-studies expert reveals that memory of crime stories with the suspects' pictures reflects racial stereotypes, and African Americans are especially likely to be mistakenly identified as perpetrators of violent crimes. When readers were asked to identify criminal suspects pictured in stories about violent crimes, they were more prone to misidentify African Americans than white suspects. The same readers, to a far lesser degree, tended to link white offenders more with nonviolent crime. Essentially, people's mismemories of violent crime new seem to implicate all black men rather than the specific individuals who are actually pictured. In essence, the Penn State findings support the notion that stereotypes of black men as violent criminals are reflected in what people recall from news reports. This kind of mismemory has many implications ranging from issues related to law enforcement to issues related to everyday activities such as greater fear or distrust of others. In addition, the study indicates that self-reported racial attitudes, no matter how prejudiced or enlightened, had no impact on participants' ability to correctly identify the race of a criminal suspect. This suggests that whites may not realize the degree to which deeply imbedded stereotypes tamper with their memories.[13]

The images associated with other racial groups tend to be crime specific. For instance, the image of Asian criminality is related to Asian gangs. Their crimes are viewed primarily as a reflection of internal group conflict. The public picture of Latinos and crime most closely resembles that of blacks. Latinos, too, are viewed as stealthy and criminal. They, however, are not perceived as posing the same kind of criminal threat as blacks. Latinos, like Asians, tend to be viewed as involved in intra-racial crimes. American Indians are stereotypically portrayed as committing vice-related crimes such as alcohol-related crime and gambling. American Indian crimes are also typically portrayed as intra-group offenses.[14]

It is interesting that, as a group, whites have managed to escape being associated with crime. This would not be so odd if whites were not responsible, in raw numbers, for most of the crime that is committed. Each year, whites account for almost seventy percent of the total arrests, and today they comprise about forty percent of the prison population. When the media does connect someone white with a crime, for example serial murderer Jeffrey Dahmer, it does not implicate the entire white race. It is notable that phrases such as "white crime" and "white-on-white" crime are not part of our public lexicon on crime.

In addition, many sociologists have argued that the mass media promote narrow definitions of who people are and what they can be. What is considered beauty, for example, is not universal. Ideals of beauty change as cultures change, and depend on what certain cultural institutions promote as beautiful. Aging is not beautiful, youth is. Light skin is promoted as more beautiful than dark skin (regardless of one's race) although being tanned is seen as more beautiful than being pale. In African American women's magazines, the models typified as most beautiful are generally those with clearly Anglo features—light skin, blue eyes, and straight or wavy hair. These depictions have fluctuated over time. In the early 1970s, for example, there was a more Afrocentric ideal of beauty—darker skin, "afro" hairdos, and African clothing. Today, the images of African American women have returned to more Eurocentric depictions of beauty. European facial features are also pervasive in the images of Asian and Latino women appearing in U.S. magazines. The media communicate that only certain forms of beauty are culturally valued. These ideals are not somehow "natural"; rather, they are constructed by those who control cultural and economic institutions.[15]

Images of women and African American males in the media are similarly limiting. Content analyses of television (TV) reveal that, during prime time, white men are a large majority of the characters shown. On soap operas, women are cast either as evil or good but naïve. In music videos, women characters appear less frequently, have more beautiful bodies, are more physically attractive, wear more sexy and skimpy clothing, and are more often the object of another's gaze than their male counterparts.[16] An increase has been evident in the extent to which women are depicted in professional jobs, but such images usually depict professional women as young, suggesting that career success comes early, especially to thin and beautiful women.[17] Media images distort the realities of gender roles for men, too. For example, in television commercials men appearing alone with children (that is, without a spouse present) are more likely to be shown outside, less likely to be doing household chores, more likely to be shown with boys, and seldom shown with infants. Although such portrayals show men as involved in family life, they still project stereotypical norms of fatherhood.[18] Also, whereas nurturing images of men are now more frequent in the media, they are most likely to appear in magazines read by women.[19]

Even though African Americans and Latinos watch more television than whites do, they are a small proportion of TV characters, generally confined to a narrow variety of character types and depicted in stereotypical ways.[20] Latinos are often stereotyped as criminals or passionate lovers. African American men are most typically seen as criminals, athletes, sports commentators, or entertainers; African American women are shown in domestic or sexual roles or as sex objects. It is difficult to find a single show in which Asians are the principal characters—usually they are depicted in silent roles as domestics or other behind-the-scenes or sidekick characters. American Indians make occasional appearances in which they usually are depicted as mystics or warriors. Typically, if presented at all, American Indians are marginal characters stereotyped as silent, exotic, and mysterious. Jewish women are generally invisible on popular TV programming, except when they are ridiculed in stereotypical roles.[21] Class stereotypes abound, as well, with working-class men typically portrayed as being ineffectual, even buffoonish.[22] Working-class men are most likely seen in beer commercials or police shows.[23] On television, people of color are also far more likely to be found in comedies than dramas. African American women, especially, are most typically seen as characters in comedy shows. In dramas, African American and Latino men are typically the sidekicks, not the major characters.

Women and racial or ethnic minorities are also seriously underrepresented in and on network news, one of the most important outlets of information about society and culture. Although women's representation among network news reporters has increased, they constitute only fifteen percent of network news reporters and twenty percent of print journalists (although they compose sixty-eight percent of journalism school graduates). Men write two-thirds of the front-page stories in the news and provide eighty-five percent of television reporting. Only three percent of newspaper executives are women.

Women of color are even further underrepresented, providing only two percent of broadcast media stories. Men also provide eighty-five percent of quotes or references in the media, are seventy-five percent of those interviewed on TV, and are ninety percent of the most-cited pundits—even on issues that involve women.[24] With limited coverage of issues important to women and to racial or ethnic groups, the public can hardly be well informed about gender and race as social and political issues. This has led sociologists to conclude that the news media reflect the white male social order and primarily support the "public, business, and professional upper middle-class sectors of society."[25] It is therefore not surprising that many minorities are dissatisfied with how they see themselves represented in the media.

A television trend that was very popular during the 1990s and portrayed crude, one-dimensional images of African Americans was the proliferation of daytime talk shows. These shows often featured black guests who talked in loud, profane language or Ebonics, for example; used animated gestures, and freely discussed their criminal involvement or sexual liaisons, sometimes both. Most talk shows, current and canceled—hosted by Jerry Springer, Ricki Lake, Montel Williams, Tempestt Bledsoe, Richard Bey, Sally Jessy Raphael, Mark Walberg, Rolonda Watts, Charles Perez, Jenny Jones, Maury Povich, Gordon Elliot, and Geraldo Rivera—portray blacks as amoral buffoons, sassy single mothers, arrogant absent fathers, and unfaithful friends. A common feature of these shows is a disproportionately high number of blacks and Latino guests.[26]

Television is not the only form of popular culture that influences public consciousness about gender and race. Music, film, books, and other industries play a significant role in molding public consciousness. What images are produced by these cultural forms? Countless studies document the persistence of race, gender, and age stereotypes in various forms of popular culture. Rock videos depict men as the center of attention or show white women as trying to get the attention of men. Greeting cards ridicule the process of aging. Try, for example, to buy a greeting card that does not stereotype older women or older men. Women's magazines send endless messages about women's body image. A recent analysis comparing women's and men's magazines finds that seventy-eight percent of women's-magazine covers contain a message regarding bodily appearance, usually suggesting that losing weight will lead to a better life; men's magazines focus on providing entertainment, expanding knowledge, and learning hobbies or other activities.[27] Newspapers describe women athletes by comparing them with men or providing commentary that has little to do with an athlete's performance.[28] Even the new world of cyberspace depicts images and activities based on cultural stereotypes.[29] Consider Mattel computers sold only a few years ago: blue for boys, pink for girls. The boys' computer is named *Hot Wheels*; the girls', *Barbie PC*. The boys' model comes with a *Hot Wheels* steering wheel and pedals; the girls, with a pink digital camera. Although identical in computing hardware, the boys' model comes with twelve educational software packages; the girls', only six. Furthermore, the boys' software includes three packages designed to increase math skills, the girls', only one. And, whereas the boys' model includes a human anatomy program that also teaches three-dimensional graphics, the girls' includes various fashion design and photography packages.

Do these images matter? Studies find that exposure to traditional sexual imagery in music videos has an effect on college students' attitudes about adversarial sexual relationships.[30] Other studies find that even when viewers see media images as unrealistic, they think that others find the images important and will evaluate them accordingly. This has been found especially to be true for young white girls who think boys will judge them by how well they match the media ideal.[31] Although people do not just passively internalize media images, and do distinguish between fantasy and reality,[32] such images form cultural ideals that have a huge impact on people's behavior, values, and self-image. This is a very important point for understanding why African American males are often portrayed as criminals.

OUTLINE OF THE BOOK

This book discusses the role of history and, more important, prejudices, discrimination, stereotypes, and racism in understanding contemporary media depictions of the African American male criminal stereotype. One contention is that a racist society needs racist ideologies to reinforce racial superiority. These ideologies sometimes manifest themselves through popular discourse such as mass media. Also presented is a schema, *conceptual entrapment by media imagery*, that illustrates the rationale for depicting African American males as criminals. More specifically, television and the daily newspaper are used to illustrate how the dominant society depiction of the African American male as criminal has achieved prominence in prime-time mainly due to increased quantity and improved quality of such available programs as live reenactments of suspected criminals. Notwithstanding, in a 1995 report by the University of California Television Violence Monitoring Project, prime-time television has devoted at least two-thirds of its time to crime.[33]

Also, in an earlier study by Carolyn Stroman in which she discusses televised crime in the 1980s, she suggests that there are three major expectations for television crime shows currently on the air. First, there has traditionally been an overemphasis on violent crime. Second, there has been an overrepresentation of African American criminals and underrepresentation of African American victims of crime.[34] Third, crime on television is almost always unsuccessful because officers are most likely unable to apprehend all suspected criminals.[35]

Moreover, Estep and MacDonald found that during prime time, twenty-two percent of all crimes depicted were murder, very often overemphasizing violence on television. The typical suspect arrested for murder is a young, lower-class male, and most likely an African American. Thus, the only dimension on which television is accurate for murder suspects is their sex. On television, half of all murder suspects arrested by police are African American, suggesting unequivocally that television has a long way to go before achieving an accurate portrayal of murder suspects.[36]

Sociologists Robert Staples and Terry Jones state in an article that the media has typically operated negatively for groups at the bottom rung of the social strata. As the most oppressed of the exploited classes, African Americans have been portrayed in the media in ways that reinforce the image of white superiority and black inferiority, the purpose of which has been the stabilization of status quo relations among the races. In their view, the mass accessibility of television has multiplied the negative media image of African Americans a thousand fold.[37]

Also, Staples and Jones have maintained that the people who control what is shown on TV seem to believe that whites feel most comfortable with blacks playing the roles of fools, maids, funny men and small-time hustlers. Moreover, the authors provided evidence to suggest that African Americans are generally stereotyped, with forty-nine percent of all African Americans playing roles of criminals, servants, entertainers or athletes. To them, the demeaning stereotypes of black characterizations have become common place and have won out over multidimensional African American humanity. Prime time, their study underscored, has been a living monument to the media industry's inability or unwillingness to portray African American characters as whole human beings. Its continual portrayal of African Americans in demeaning roles has had a negative impact on both African Americans and white America. To understand white America's need to denigrate black America, it is necessary to examine white cultural ideology and its relationship to the television industry. Staples and Jones wrote that "it appears that the greater the distance between cultures, the greater the room for misinterpretation, distortions, or negative perceptions to develop."[38]

Similar to television, news coverage is yet another major source of information on crime that influences society in defining what crime is and who is a criminal. Existing research examining news coverage of the African American community reveals disturbing biases and patterns of blatant distortion at the hands of the nation's largest and most respected print and broadcast media. Indeed, some analysts warn that the power that once toppled a president—in the case of Richard Nixon—now works the equivalent on the African American community. It is also suggested that the power is thwarting African American social advancement by conveying the illusion of impartial reporting while applying vastly different standards to news coverage of whites and African Americans. Young people, both African American and white, may be at a particular risk of internalizing these misconceptions because their experience leaves them ill equipped to challenge news reports.

Hence, biased reporting could easily be used by the average reader to develop an unreal description of African Americans. For example, a 1990 survey of 3,125 news stories collected at random over a one-month period in Boston revealed striking differences in news coverage from white- and African American–owned media outlets. In the white media, eighty-five percent of the news about Boston's predominantly African American neighborhoods reinforced negative stereotypes of African Americans as being prone to violence and crime and unable to maintain cohesive families. In contrast, news from the African American media—comprising stories from the same neighborhoods and collected over the same thirty-day period—depicted the African American community with more balance, reporting entrepreneurial breakthroughs, drug arrests, high academic achievement, classroom problems, successful campaigns to remedy poor living conditions, and community malaise. The positive stories rarely appeared in the white-owned media.[39]

In the region, whose African American community totals twenty-five percent of the population (with a twenty-two percent African American population in Boston proper),[40] the study also found a persistent tendency for white reporters to seek out white experts for comments, even on such issues of vital concern to the African American community as unemployment. Boston's white-owned media outlets displayed reluctance to cite racism as an underlying factor in news events ranging from white-on-black harassment to educational disparities to employment discrimination. The study concluded that whereas the white media portray themselves through their charitable work and public-service announcements as advocating racial harmony, their news coverage perpetuates racism by reinforcing common negative assumptions about African Americans, failing to show positive African American role models, and neglecting to discuss racism as an important social force.

In fact, in a more recent study conducted by the Berkeley Media Studies Group and the Justice Policy Institute, researchers found that news organizations exaggerate the proportion of minorities and young people who commit crimes, thus profoundly misinforming the public. If news audiences take crime coverage at face value, they are likely to believe—falsely—that most crime is extremely violent and that perpetrators are black, victims are white, and young people are dangerous. "It is not just that African Americans are overrepresented as criminals and underrepresented as victims, or that young people are overrepresented as criminals, or that violent crime itself is given undue coverage," the researchers conclude; "It is that all three occur together, combining forces to produce a terribly unfair and inaccurate overall image of crime in America."[41] Homicide coverage on network news increased a striking 473 percent from 1990 to 1998 while homicides dropped thirty-three percent, the researchers found, stressing that minorities, especially blacks, are disproportionately portrayed as perpetrators of crime.[42]

In the second half of this book, implications of depicting African American males as criminals are discussed, including the often negative and criminal role of African Americans in Hollywood major movies; and the adverse affects of "gangsta rap" music and racial profiling, or "driving while black," just to name a few effects. These negative depictions of African Americans help set the stage for similar law-and-order films for the following decades, and acted to help reinforce a stereotype of the lethal "African American criminal." Such negative media perceptions of African Americans were functional in that they helped Republican George H. W. Bush win the 1988 U.S. presidential election. Bush used manipulative television "sound bites" to exploit the crimes of black furloughed rapist Willie Horton.

Such media racism helped foster public perceptions that, in part, lead social scientist T. J. Gibbs to conclude that young black males in America are "an endangered species." Gibbs pointed out that "Black males are portrayed by mass media in a limited number of roles, most often deviant, dangerous, and dysfunctional.[43]

NOTES

1. Laura T. Fishman. 2002. "The Black Bogeyman and White Self-Righteousness," in Coramae Richey Mann and Marjorie S. Zatz (Eds.), *Images of Color: Images of Crime*, 2nd ed. (Los Angeles, CA: Roxbury), 177.

2. Ibid., 181.

3. This is not a trivial point. Some conservative writers attribute black American disadvantage entirely or in part to purported patterns of "social pathology" said to be characteristic of "black culture." Yet, even if that were so—and the point is eminently arguable—such "pathology" could not be rightly understood as an alien cultural blemish imposed on an otherwise pristine Euro-American canvas. Rather, it could only be seen as a domestic product, made over the generations wholly in the "good old USA," for which the entire nation bears a responsibility. Clearly, this would not be the case—at least, not to the same degree—if there were to be found any comparable, adverse cultural patterns among, say, Chinese, Italian, or Korean immigrants.

4. United States Department of Health and Human Services, *2001 Survey on National Drug Abuse*, 69.

5. See, especially, Dennis M. Rome. 2002. "Murderers, Rapists, and Drug Addicts," in Coramae Richey Mann and Majorie S. Zatz (Eds.), *Images of Color, Images of Crime* (Los Angeles, CA: Roxbury), 71–82.

6. Frederick Douglass. *The Life and Times of Frederick Douglass* (New York: Crowell Publishers, 1966).

7. University of Maryland, 2000 General Social Survey.

8. See, especially, Glenn C. Loury. *The Anatomy of Racial Inequality* (Cambridge, MA: Harvard University Press, 2002).

9. Peter Berger and Thomas Luckmann. *The Social Construction of Reality: A Treatise in the Sociology of Knowledge* (New York: Anchor Books, 1966); Richard Quinney. *The Social Reality of Crime* (Boston: Little, Brown, 1970).

10. Katheryn K. Russell. *The Color of Crime: Racial Hoaxes, White Fear, Black Protectionism, Police Harassment, and Other Macroaggressions* (New York: New York University Press, 1998), xiii.

11. Russell, *The Color of Crime*, xiii.

12. For one assignment in my Introduction to Criminal Justice seminar taught during fall 2002, students were asked to use either photographs or pictures to best illustrate their definition of crime. One student had children in a preschool class draw a picture of what they perceived as crime. Several of these children drew pictures that included criminals dressed in traditional "criminal grab" such as ski masks; although some of the criminals were drawn with ski masks, the preschool children still identified the criminal as "black, Hispanic or American Indian."

13. Mary Beth Oliver and Dana Fonash, "Race and Crime in the News: Whites' Identification and Misidentification of Violent and Nonviolent Criminal Suspects," *Journal of Media Psychology* (vol. 14, no. 2: May, 2002): 137–156.

14. These stereotypes will be discussed more fully in the latter half of the book.

15. See, especially, Scott Kassell. "Afrocentrism and Eurocentrism in African American Magazine Ads," Unpublished senior thesis (Princeton: Princeton University, 1995); Naomi Wolf. *The Beauty Myth: How Images of Beauty Are Used Against*

Women (New York: William Morrow, 1991); Diane Barthel. *Putting on Appearances: Gender and Advertising* (Philadelphia: Temple University Press, 1988); Wendy Chapkis. *Beauty Secrets: Women and the Politics of Appearance* (Boston: South End Press, 1986); Michael Leslie. "Slow Fade to? Advertising in Ebony Magazine, 1957–1989," *Journalism and Mass Communication Quarterly* 72 (summer 1995): 426–435.

16. See, for example, Nancy Signorielli, Douglas McLeod, and Elaine Healy. "Gender Stereotypes in MTV Commercials: The Beat Goes On," *Journal of Broadcasting and Electronic Media* 38 (winter 1994): 91–101; Lisa J. Sloat. "Incubus: Male Songwriters' Portrayals of Women's Sexuality in Pop Metal Music," in Jonathon S. Epstein (Ed.), *Youth Culture: Identity in a Postmodern World* (Malden, MA: Blackwell, 1998), 286–301.

17. Nancy Signorielli and Aaron Bruce. "Recognition and Respect: A Content Analysis of Prime-Time Television Characters Across Three Decades," *Sex Roles* 40 (April 1999): 527–544.

18. See, especially, Gayle Kaufman. "The Portrayal of Men's Family Roles in Television Commercials," *Sex Roles* 41(September 1999): 439–458.

19. See Anthony Vigorito and Timothy Curry. "Marketing Masculinity: Gender Identity and Popular Magazines." *Sex Roles*. 39(July): 135-152.

20. Richard T. Schaefer, *Racial and Ethnic Groups* (Upper Saddle River, NJ: Prentice Hall, 2000): 64–68.

21. See Susan Kray. "Orientalization of an 'Almost White' Woman: The Interlocking Effects of Race, Class, Gender, and Ethnicity in American Mass Media." *Critical Studies in Mass Communication* 10 (December 1993): 349–366.

22. For example, Richard Butsch. "Class and Gender in Four Decades of Television Situation Comedy," *Critical Studies in Mass Communication* 9 (September 1992): 387–399; Gail Dines and Jean M. Humez, eds. *Gender, Race and Class in Media: A Text Reader* (Thousand Oaks, CA: Sage Publications, 1995).

23. See Julie Bettie. "Class Dismissed? Roseanne and the Changing Face of Working-Class Iconography," *Social Text* 45 (winter 1995): 125–149.

24. Deborah Rhode. "Media Images, Feminist Issues," *Signs* 20 (spring 1995): 685–710.

25. See, especially, Herbert Gans. *Deciding What's News: A Study of the CBS Evening News, NBC Nightly News, Newsweek and Time* (New York: Pantheon, 1979).

26. Russell, p. 2.

27. See, especially, Amy Malkin, Kimberlie Wornian, and Joan C. Chrisler. "Women and Weight: Gendered Messages on Magazine Covers." *Sex Roles* 40 (April 1999): 647–655.

28. See Ray Jones, Audrey Murrell, and Jennifer Jackson. "Pretty versus Powerful in the Sports Pages: Print Media Coverage of U.S. Women's Olympic Gold Medal Winning Teams." *Journal of Sport and Social Issues* 23 (May 1999): 183–192.

29. See Bosah Ebo, (Ed.). *Cyberghetto or Cybertopia? Race, Class and Gender on the Internet.* (Westport, CT: Praeger, 1998).

30. See Linda Kalof. "The Effects of Gender and Music Video Imagery on Sexual Attitudes." *Journal of Social Psychology* 139 (June 1999): 378–385.

31. See Melissa Milkie. "Social Comparisons, Reflected Appraisals, and Mass Media: The Impact of Pervasive Beauty Images on Black and White Girls' Self-Concepts." *Social Psychology Quarterly* 62 (June 1999): 190–210.

32. For example, Dawn Currie. "Decoding Femininity: Advertisements and Their Teenage Readers." *Gender and Society* 11 (August 1997): 453–477.

33. University of California, Los Angeles. Television Monitoring Project, 1995, 69.

34. See, for example, Steven Chermak and Alexander Weiss. "The News Value of African American Victims: An Examination of the Media's Presentation of Homicide," *Journal of Crime and Justice* 21(2) 1998: 71–88.

35. Carolyn Stroman. "Media Use and Perceptions of Crime," *Journalism Quarterly* 62 (Summer 1998): 340–345.

36. R. Estep and P. T. MacDonald. "How Prime Time Crime Evolved on TV, 1976–1981," *Journalism Quarterly* 60 (1983): 293–300.

37. Robert Staples and Terry Jones. "Culture, Ideology and Black Television Images," *The Black Scholar* 16 (3) 1985: 10–20.

38. Ibid.

39. As cited in Kirk Johnson. "Objective News and Other Myths: The Poisoning of Young Black Minds," *Journal of Negro Education* 60 (3) 1991: 328–341.

40. United States Census Bureau, 2000 Census.

41. Lori Dorfman and Vincent Schiraldi. *Off Balance: Youth, Race and Crime in the News* (Washington, DC: The Berkeley Media Studies Group and the Justice Policy Institute, 2001).

42. Ibid.

43. T. J. Gibbs. *Young, Black, and Male in America: An Endangered Species* (Dover, MA: Auburn House, 1988), 2.

Brief Historical
Overview of African Americans

First, those who managed the slaves had to maintain strict discipline. One master said, "Unconditional submission is the only footing upon which slavery should be placed." Another said, "The slave must know that his master is to govern absolutely and he is to obey implicitly, that he is never, for a moment, to exercise either his will or judgment in opposition to a positive order." Second, the masters felt that they had to implant in the bondsman a consciousness of personal inferiority. This sense of inferiority was deliberately extended to his past. The slave owners were convinced that in order to control the Negroes, the slaves "had to feel that African ancestry tainted them, that their color was a badge of degradation." The third step in the training process was to awe the slaves with a sense of the masters' enormous power. It was necessary, various owners said, "to make them stand in fear." The fourth aspect was to attempt to "persuade the bondsman to take an interest in the master's enterprise and to accept the standards of good conduct." Thus the master's criteria of what was good and true and beautiful were to be accepted unquestioningly by the slaves. The final step, according to Stampp's documents, was "to impress Negroes with their helplessness: to create in them a habit of perfect dependence upon their masters."

Here, then, was the way to produce a perfect slave. Accustom him to rigid discipline, demand from him unconditional submission, impress upon him *a sense of his innate inferiority, develop in him a paralyzing fear of white men, train him to adopt the master's code of good behavior, and instill in him a sense of complete dependence.*[1]

One cannot discuss how the criminal stereotype of the African American male is used today—specifically how, even as we begin the twenty-first century, some persons will promote false allegations that attribute the most egregious conduct to African Americans because they believe that the public will unhesitatingly accept such stories—without placing this precept[2] of inferiority in a historical context. The public perception of African Americans as inferior provides the basis of acceptability for the most outrageous lies. This chapter begins with an historical overview because there is a direct correlation between the colonial period and perceptions today.

OPERATIONAL DEFINITIONS OF RACE

Throughout this study, I will employ a definition of race posited by Glenn Loury:

[Race is] a cluster of inheritable bodily markings carried by a largely endogamous group of individuals, markings that can be observed by others with ease, that can be changed or misrepresented only with great difficulty, and that have come to be invested in a particular society at a given historical moment with social meaning.[3]

It is important to point out that Loury maintains that no biologically defined races exist in the human species—hence, because "race" is socially and culturally defined, by "deconstructing race" one can begin to understand why African American males are often depicted as criminals in mass media. A good starting point is to understand two terms: majority and minority groups. Historian Louis Aptheker noted that a racist society breeds and needs a racist writing of historical literature to support and reinforce the ideologies of racial superiority.[4] We might extend that idea to suggest that a racist society also requires a racist media to disseminate these values and beliefs to a mass audience. In an attempt to motivate the predominantly African American student audience, media magnate Ted Turner spoke at Howard University. Turner maintained that African Americans or "Afro-Americans," as he puts it, are not minorities. Rather, he argued that Anglos are in fact the real minorities. Turner said that there are more nonwhites than whites on this planet, making whites the real minority.[5]

Although Turner was attempting to affirm a high level of self-esteem in his predominantly African American student audience members, by suggesting that the "minority" label has a negative connotation may be misleading to these students. According to many social scientists, the term *minority group* implies the existence of a majority group, a dominant group with superior resources and rights. This points up differences in power among groups and underscores racial and ethnic stratification, a hierarchy of more- or less-powerful groups. It is perhaps more accurate to use the term *dominant group* for a majority group, as well as *subordinate group* for a minority group because a majority group can be numerically a minority, as is the case with the ruling white Europeans in a number of colonial societies.[6] The point here is that when a person with the power, media influence, and prestige of Ted Turner makes such inaccurate statements, this convolution of semantics, whether intentional or not, will only add to the confusion of the dynamics of dominant and subordinate relations. Keep in mind, however, that Ted Turner is the same person who defended Atlanta Braves fans for doing the "Tomahawk Chop," a behavior during ball games during which Atlanta Braves fans make fake American Indian sounds and move their forearms in a chopping manner. Turner defended this behavior even in light of the fact that several American Indians came forward and said that they found the Tomahawk Chop to be offensive.

Minorities are racial or ethnic groups, but not all racial or ethnic groups are minorities. Irish Americans, for example, are not now minorities, although they once were in the early part of the twentieth century. A minority group is any distinct group in society that shares common group characteristics and is forced to occupy low status in society because of prejudice and discrimination. A group may be a minority on the basis of ethnicity, race, sexual preference, age, or class status, for example. A minority group is not necessarily a numerical minority but holds low status relative to other groups in society— regardless of the size of the group. In South Africa, blacks outnumber whites ten to one, but until Nelson Mandela's election as president and the dramatic change of government in 1994, blacks were an officially oppressed and politically excluded social minority under the infamous apartheid system of government. The group that assigns a racial or ethnic group to subordinate status in society is called the dominant group or social majority. In general, a racial or ethnic minority group has the following characteristics:

1. It possesses characteristics that are popularly regarded as different from those of the dominant group (such as race, ethnicity, sexual preference, age, or religion).
2. It suffers prejudice and discrimination by the dominant group.

3. Membership in the group is frequently ascribed rather than achieved, although either form of status can be the basis for being identified as a minority.

4. Members of a minority group feel a strong sense of group solidarity. There is a "consciousness of kind" or "we" feeling. This bond grows from common cultural heritage and the shared experience of being the recipient of prejudice and discrimination.

5. Minority-group marriages are typically, although not always, among members of the same group.[7]

Based on this definition, Ted Turner is hardly a minority. In fact, Ted Turner is a member of the less than five percent of the U.S. population that controls over fifty-six percent of its wealth. In light of this fact, one is hard pressed to believe Turner's assertion that he is a minority.[8]

In his seminal work, Joseph Graves reminds us that there are at least seven ways in which racism and discrimination lead to dysfunction in a society and explain, in part, why subordinate members are sometimes vilified in mass media:

1. Discriminatory practices prevent society from making use of the contributions of all individuals. Discrimination limits the search for talent and leadership to the dominant group. Racists may also view "inferior" people as a physical resource to be apportioned in the social division of labor for the benefit of the "superior" race.[9]

2. Discrimination aggravates social problems such as poverty, delinquency, and crime and places the financial burden of alleviating these problems on the dominant group.[10]

3. Racism requires society to invest a good deal of time and money to defend the social and institutional barriers that prevent the full participation of all members.[11]

4. Racial prejudice and discrimination undercut diplomatic relations among nations. They also negatively affect efforts to increase global trade.[12]

5. Racism restricts communication among groups. Little accurate knowledge of minorities and their culture is available to the society at large.

6. Racism inhibits social change because change may assist a subordinate group.[13]

7. Discrimination promotes disrespect for law enforcement and for the peaceful settlement of disputes.[14]

Throughout the present text, the terms *racism* (the perception and/or treatment of a racial or ethnic group, or member of that group, as intellectually, socially, and culturally inferior to one's own group), *stereotype, prejudice,* and *discrimination* are used. For clarity and consistency, the following working definitions will be employed in the present study. *Stereotype* is an exaggerated belief, image or distorted truth about a person or group—a generalization that allows for little or no individual differences or social variation. Stereotypes are based on images in mass media, or on reputations passed on by parents, peers, and many other members of society. A *prejudice* is an opinion, prejudgment, or attitude about a group or its individual members. A prejudice can be positive, but in this text prejudice refers to a negative attitude. Prejudices are often accompanied by ignorance, fear or hatred. Prejudices are formed by a complex psychological process that begins with attachment to a close circle of acquaintances or an "in-group" such as a family. Prejudice, when it develops, is often aimed at "out-groups." *Discrimination* is behavior that treats people unequally because of their group memberships. Discriminatory behavior, ranging from trivial to hate crimes, often begins with negative stereotypes and prejudices.

ORIGIN OF THE INFERIOR STEREOTYPE OF AFRICAN AMERICANS

The history of African Americans began in 1619 when they arrived in the new world as captured indentured servants aboard a Dutch frigate; shortly thereafter, the status of these Africans arriving in the new world became that of captured slaves. For the next 300 years, Africans—men, women, and children—were transported to the West to labor on the rice, cotton, and sugar plantations, thus directly participating in the making of America.[15] This new status of chattel slaves—owned by plantation barons and without the rights of human beings—was very important because it shaped the way African Americans would be perceived after they received their freedom in the United States. With the ending of the Civil War, slaves were given their freedom. All through the period of U.S. history from that time up through the turn of the century, these former slaves struggled to gain the rights accorded a free people, with only a modicum of success.

Although social scientists such as Orlando Patterson remind us that slavery is not unique to North America or Europeans, it is important to point out that the precept of inferiority is unique to the American slavery experience.[16] Moreover, this experience of African Americans is unique in African Americans' ascription to inferior status in that no other ethnic minority group entered the country as slaves and, just as important, no other group was victimized across centuries the way African Americans have been victimized. The fallout from all this is that the African American and white relationship has always been one of intense conflicts as African Americans have tried to adjust to the dictates of living in a predominantly white society.[17] Bart Landry reminds us

that primarily because of their racial attitudes, whites of all classes have historically reserved the worst jobs in the economy for black workers. It is true that, with the exception of work in the slave economy, whites have at times performed these same tasks in the urban economy. Yet these menial jobs were always viewed as temporary positions in the class structure, stepping stones toward a better life for themselves or their children higher up the class ladder. These white workers, immigrant and native, did in fact move up to better jobs, or at least were able to see their sons and daughters securing better jobs than their own in the next generation. Each new generation of European immigrants competed for positions in the economy and moved a little further up the class ladder. This competition for desirable work, however, was open to whites alone. The norms of the market dictated that throughout the economy black workers be denied opportunities to compete equally with whites for desirable positions. Rather, black workers—both male and female—were reserved for the most menial labor at the very bottom of the class structure: unskilled labor and domestic work. This was not a *reserve labor pool* to be drawn upon by employers to undercut the price of white labor in semiskilled and skilled work. It was a system that defined some jobs as *colored jobs* and others as *white jobs*.[18]

By the latter part of the seventeenth century, the colonists would have in place a sort of "social and color ladder," occupied at the top rungs by propertied whites, in the middle by the poor and servant whites, and at the bottom rungs by American Indians and African American slaves.[19] Through the operation of this social and color ladder, the ruling class of whites was assured the loyalty of the poor and servant whites, on whose loyalty the fate of the colony depended, without the ruling class having to share its wealth and power with the servant class. For the poor and servant whites, the rewards for their loyalty were the somewhat illusory promise that they too could ascend to the top rungs of the ladder occupied by the propertied whites and, much more important, the eternal guarantee that they could never fall to the lower rungs occupied by the American Indians, or the lowest rungs occupied by the African Americans.

Throughout the eighteenth and nineteenth centuries until 1965, the social and color ladder was reinforced by slaveholders, legislators, and judges who articulated and perfected the rationale of black inferiority and white superiority. Evidence of this is presented by eminent legal scholars A. Leon Higginbotham, Jr. and Derrick Bell when they cite the words of South Carolina Senator James Henry Hammond in 1861:

In all social systems there must be a class to do the menial duties, to perform the drudgery of life. That is, a class requiring but a low order of intellect and but little skill. Its requisites are vigor, docility, fidelity. Such a class you must have, or you would not have that other class which leads progress, civilization, and refinement. It constitutes the very mudsill of society and of political government. . . . Fortunately for the South, she has found a race adapted to that purpose at her hand. A race inferior to her own, but eminently qualified in temper, in vigor, in docility, in capacity to stand the climate, to answer all her purposes. We use them for our purpose, and we call them slaves.[20]

African Americans have family trees in the United States extending back to the 1600s, well before the American Revolution. They are among the oldest settlers in North America, far older as a group than many prominent white immigrant groups. There is a tragic irony here. That a people who have been here as long as the first European settlers should still find themselves so discriminated against, so unwelcome in many traditionally white institutions and places, is a fact of life that is problematic both for assimilation and for the future of this ostensibly democratic nation.

The precept of inferiority for African Americans includes being singled out for having dark skin; early accounts include dark skin as being described as unusual or ugly. By 1800, blackness was seen as a critical means of sorting out people; the terms *black* and *Negro* underscored the importance of color. By the mid-1800s, advocates of slavery were arguing for acceptance of the supposed apelike characteristics of the African American, a stereotype applied by Anglo-Saxons to Irish Americans a decade or two earlier. Samuel Cartwright, in a famous article published in the 1850s, wrote that Africans were a different species than Europeans "because the head and face are anatomically constructed more after the fashion of the simiadiae" (apes).[21]

By the turn of the century, this way of insulting African Americans had taken on ludicrous forms. A low point was probably reached in 1906 when the New York Zoological Society put a small African, Ota Benga, in a cage in the monkey house of the Bronx Park Zoo as part of an exhibit. Thousands came to view the African's new home. Some African American ministers protested the degrading exhibition, but white officials as well as the white populace thought it to be very entertaining.[22]

African Americans were also charged with being mentally and morally inferior. Slavery advocates tried hard to depict slaves as childlike, happy-go-lucky *sambos*; this stereotype did not die with slavery. Between 1900 and

World War II, prominent white scientists such as geneticist Edward East of Harvard University took the position that "mentally the African negro is childlike, normally affable and cheerful, but subject to fits of fierce passion."[23]

Early discussions of African Americans' inferiority assumed that African Americans had a small brain and a lower mental capacity than that of Europeans. Southern apologists for slavery embraced views of racial inferiority, views routinely legitimated in the scientific racism of nineteenth-century writers in Europe. A burst of interest in this argument for mental inferiority occurred around 1900, when a number of American scientists argued for the inferiority of certain racial groups, including Americans of southern European and African descent. Many observers, relying heavily on intelligence quotient (IQ) tests, attempted to prove that southern and eastern Europeans were mentally inferior; others used the same tests to the same end with African Americans. Scholarly journals and popular magazines parroted this theme. Anti-black thought was coupled with theories of northern European racial superiority to other groups, southern European as well as to African. Even American presidents have participated in the crude racial theorizing since the last decades of the nineteenth century.[24]

In sum, the rationale for the precept of inferiority was this: blacks, for reasons of physiology, culture, behavior, and even religion, were something less than fully human and were therefore inferior to whites. As such, blacks could be enslaved by whites, not only because of the economic benefits that the raw physical attributes of blacks would bring whites in their efforts to turn the primitive American land into a civilized nation, but also because of the moral benefits that dominance by whites would bring blacks in soothing their ungodly instincts. If, however, the civilizing restraints of slavery were to be removed and they were free, then blacks had to be segregated from whites because, left entirely to their own devices, free blacks would tend to corrupt the moral virtue and physical purity of white society, and because the two races, one the blessed fulfillment of divine destiny, the other a cursed accident of blind evolution, could not possibly live together peacefully in society without the beneficent controlling hand of the superior race on the inferior one.

Hence, conceptions of crime and the subsequent labeling of African Americans as criminals are ways in which this form of superior/inferior ideology continues to manifest itself. Dominant society is depicting crime as something that exists mostly in the African American communities. In subsequent chapters, how and why crime is painted with a black face and how this misconception is disseminated in our society will be discussed.

UNDERSTANDING "RACE"

[Deconstructing] the idea of biological race lays bare the fallacies of racism. If biological races do not exist, then what we call "race" is the invention not of nature but of our social institutions and practices. The social nature of racial categories is significant because social practice can be altered far more readily than can genetic constitution. Although professional scientists generally agree on the fallacy of race, this idea has yet to find its way into the public discourse.[25]

Integral to a discussion of the precept of inferiority to understanding present-day media depictions of African American males as criminals is a discussion of the origin of "race." Biologically, a race may be defined as an isolated, inbreeding population with a distinctive genetic heritage. Because of human migration and interbreeding, there are few, if any, isolated and pure races left. The genes that determine racial characteristics (e.g., skin color or hair texture) have been disseminated throughout the world and exist in nearly every possible combination. For example, skin color varies in shades from one extreme to the other, and there are no clear or definite points at which black skin color stops and white (or brown or yellow or red) skin color begins.[26]

According to a 1989 survey by anthropologist Leonard Lieberman and his colleagues, about seventy percent of cultural anthropologists, and half of physical anthropologists, reject race as a biological category.[27] One argument against standard biological racial categories focuses on the fact that genes of individuals within racial groups are actually very different. In 1972, Richard Lewontin of Harvard University provided evidence for the genetic case against race. Analyzing seventeen genetic markers in 168 populations such as Austrians, Thais, and Apaches, he found that there is more genetic difference within one race than there is between that race and another. Only 6.3 percent of the genetic differences could be explained by the individuals' belonging to different races. That is, if any two blacks walking along the street are chosen randomly, and their twenty-three pairs of chromosomes are analyzed, one might find that their genes have less in common than do the genes of one of them with that of a random white person.[28]

More recently, the Human Genome Diversity Project used 1990s genetics to extend Lewontin's analysis. It concluded that genetic variation from one individual to another of the same race deluges the average differences between racial groupings. The more we learn about humankind's genetic differences, says geneticist Luca Cavalli-Sforza of Stanford University, who chairs the committee that directs the biodiversity project, the more we see that they have almost nothing to do with what we call race.

If race is a valid biological concept, anyone in any culture should be able to look at any individual and say, "You are a. . . ." It should not be the case, as French tennis star Yannick Noah said a few years ago, that "[I]n Africa I am white, and in France I am black." (His mother is French and his father is from Cameroon.)

Scholars who believe in the biological validity of race argue that groupings reflect human prehistory. That is, populations that evolved together, and separately from others, constitute a race. This school of thought holds that blacks should all be in one race because they are descended from people who stayed on the continent where humanity began. Asians should be another race because they are the descendants of groups who walked north and east until they reached the Pacific. Whites of the pale, blond variety should be another race because their ancestors filled Europe. Because of their appearance, these populations represent the extremes, the archetypes, of human diversity—the reds, blues and yellows from which you can make every other hue. According to F. Marks,[29] if one uses these archetypes as groups, one has classified only a very thin proportion of the world's people, which is not very useful. Marks further argues that as people walked out of Africa, they were differentiating along the way. In other words, to equate "extreme" with "primordial" is not supported by history.

Often, shared traits are a sign of shared heritage—racial heritage. According to Alice Brues, an anthropologist at the University of Colorado, shared traits are not random. Brues suggests that, within a continent, of course there are a number of variants pertaining to traits, but some are characteristic of the larger area, too. So it is natural to look for these major divisions. It simplifies the thinking. A wide distribution of traits, however, makes them suspect as evidence of a shared heritage. The dark skin of Somalis and Ghanaians, for instance, indicates that they evolved under the same selective force (a sunny climate). But that is all it shows. It does not show that they are any more closely related, in the sense of sharing more genes, than either is to Greeks. Calling Somalis and Ghanaians black, therefore, sheds no further light on their evolutionary history and implies—wrongly—that they are more closely related to each other than either is to someone of a different race. Similarly, the long noses of North Africans and northern Europeans reveal that they evolved in dry or cold climates (the nose moistens air before the air reaches the lungs, and longer noses moisten more air). The tall, thin bodies of Kenya's Massai evolved to dissipate heat; Eskimos evolved short, squat bodies to retain it. Calling these people different races adds nothing to that understanding.

Where did the three standard racial divisions come from? They entered the social, and scientific, consciousness during the Age of Exploration. Historian

Loring Brace does not think it is a coincidence that the standard races represent peoples who, as he puts it, "lived at the end of the Europeans' trade route"—in Africa and China—in the days after navigators set sail. Before Europeans took to the seas, there was little perception of races. But if the English sailor left Lisbon harbor and dropped anchor off the Kingdom of Niger, people looked so different he felt compelled to invent a scheme to explain the world—and, perhaps, distance himself from the Africans.[30]

If race is not real, how can researchers say that blacks have higher rates of infant mortality, lower rates of osteoporosis and a higher incidence of hypertension and a unique predisposition to sickle-cell anemia? Because a social construct can have biological effects. Consider hypertension among African Americans. Roughly thirty-six percent have high blood pressure, compared with about twenty-four percent of whites, but scientists have found the greatest incidence of hypertension among blacks who are upwardly mobile achievers.[31] This could be attributed to mundane interactions such as going to a bank or department store and being treated disrespectfully—this unfair treatment coincides with blacks' self-image as respectable achievers, leading to more stress and hypertension. The black upwardly mobile are more likely to encounter discriminatory white culture. Lab studies show that stressful situations—such as being followed in grocery stores as if you were a shoplifter—elevate blood pressure and lead to vascular changes that cause hypertension.[32] In this case, race captures social factors such as the experience of discrimination. Further evidence that hypertension has more to do with society than with biology: black Africans have among the lowest rates of hypertension in the world.

If we take the affliction of sickle-cell anemia, which is said to be more prevalent among African Americans, we discover that, although it does reach high frequencies in some parts of sub-Saharan Africa, it did not originate there. Its distribution includes southern Italy, the eastern Mediterranean, parts of the Middle East, and over into India. In fact, it represents a kind of adaptation that aids survival in the face of a particular kind of malaria, and wherever that malaria is a prominent threat, sickle-cell anemia tends to occur in higher frequencies. It would appear that the gene that controls that trait was introduced to sub-Saharan Africa by traders from those parts of the Middle East where it had arisen in conjunction with the conditions created by the early development of agriculture.

Another example of a social construct having biological consequences (in this case, depression) is the life of Leanita McClain. Joe Feagin and Clairece Booher Feagin describe her life thus:

In May 1984 one of this country's most talented young journalists, Leanita McClain, committed suicide. Just thirty-two years old, she had won several major journalism awards and was the first African American to serve on the *Chicago Tribune*'s editorial board. Why did such a talented black woman commit suicide? The answer is doubtless complex, but one factor looms large: the problem of coping with a culturally different, often racist, and discriminatory white world. Reviewing McClain's life, one writer has analyzed the conformity to white ways that is faced by middle-class black employees in historically white work-places:

Black women consciously choose their speech, their laughter, their walk, their mode of dress and car. They trim and straighten their hair. . . . They learn to wear a mask.

Black Americans in the corporate world not only face blatant discrimination but also suffer greatly from the subtle pressures to adapt to the values and ways of that white world.[33]

If race does not provide a significant biological explanation of illnesses, can it offer a biological explanation of something as complex as intelligence? Psychologists are among the strongest proponents of retaining the three conventional racial categories. It organizes and explains their data in the most parsimonious way, as Richard Herrnstein and Charles Murray argue in *The Bell Curve*.[34] But sociologists and anthropologists say that such conclusions are built on a foundation of sand. If nothing else, every ethnic group evolved under conditions in which intelligence was a requirement for survival. If there are intelligence genes, they must be in all ethnic groups equally; differences in intelligence must be a cultural and social artifact.

CRACKING *THE BELL CURVE*

In *The Bell Curve*, social scientists Richard Herrnstein and Charles Murray suggest that intellectuals and policy makers overlook the role intelligence plays in determining wealth, poverty, and social status.[35] More specifically, they argue that the status of blacks is influenced by the fact that they are, as a group, intellectually inferior to whites. This book has once again brought about a debate on whether intelligence and success are biologically determined.

A major criticism of Herrnstein and Murray's discourse is that they applied erroneous statistical techniques to analyze their data. The result is that their findings are flawed and overstated. Social scientists Michael Hout, Samuel Lucas and Kim Voss published a critique of *The Bell Curve* in their book entitled *Inequality by Design: Cracking the Bell Curve Myth*.[36] Hout and his associates analyze the same data cited in *The Bell Curve* but offer another explanation: social policies, not IQ, are the main reason for inequality. In other words, success is determined more by the rules of the game than by the list of participants. To understand why the United States has more inequality than any other industrialized nation, the authors say, it is important to look at health care, taxes, housing, education, and welfare policies. "It is not that low intelligence leads to inferior status; it is that inferior status leads to low intelligence-test scores."[37]

Like Herrnstein and Murray, Hout and his associates studied existing data on 12,500 Americans who were surveyed by government-sponsored researchers for more than ten years, starting in 1979.[38] In redoing the statistical analysis of these data, Hout and his associates found that Herrnstein and Murray overstated the role of IQ because of a series of errors and omissions in their study. For example, when Hout and his associates added new factors such as family structure, neighborhood, and educational, experiences into their analysis, they found that a child's social environment is a greater risk factor for poverty than his or her IQ score.

To debunk Herrnstein and Wilson's idea that whites and Asians are better off because they are smarter than blacks, Hout and his associates considered other societies in which minorities perform poorly on standardized tests. For example, Koreans do poorly on IQ tests in Japan, where that group falls at the bottom on the social ladder. But in the United States, Japanese and Koreans score about the same. A key finding of *Inequality by Design* is that in invisible ways, American policies often neglect the disadvantaged: mortgage interest deductions favor the middle class; private insurance tends to subsidize high earners; corporations benefit from tax breaks, and so on.

As a scientific manuscript, Herrnstein and Wilson's book is pseudoscientific at best. An undergraduate student presenting her senior thesis could not get away with the degree of methodological and statistical butchery that Herrnstein and Murray do. Yet, in spite of the methodological weaknesses, Herrnstein and Murray have sold hundreds of thousands of copies of their book in hardback. Why the popularity? Perhaps it is because they offer seemingly scientific support for widely held views regarding race. For example, today, many whites are likely to say "blacks have gone far enough," or "they have had their chance," and books like Herrnstein and Murray's offer evidence that can be cited in support for this position. It seems that society is increasingly willing to accept these negative views about blacks rather than recognizing that we need to work out serious solutions to serious social problems that disproportionately affect blacks. Herrnstein and Murray offer support for the view that we have done enough, and for society's rejection of discrimination as the cause of racial inequality in America today. In fact, based on public opinion polls, most whites believe that blacks should not be entitled to preferential treatment when pursuing jobs, housing, education and other societal resources.

Moreover, according to a recent Gallup poll survey, a majority of whites do not feel that discrimination exists: for example, seventy-nine percent of whites believe that a black person now has as good a chance as a white person to be hired, a jump of thirty-three percentage points since 1963. Seventy-seven percent of whites believe that blacks overestimate the amount of discrimination in America, and sixty-two percent do not believe new civil rights laws are needed to reduce discrimination against blacks.[39]

But blacks challenge this belief. Despite recognizing that the civil rights movement forced extraordinary changes beneficial to blacks, they remain nearly as dissatisfied with the state of racial equality as they were thirty years ago; less than half of blacks (forty-six percent) feel that they have a fair chance at being hired for a job for which they are qualified—twenty-two percentage points more than in 1963 (twenty-four percent), in marked contrast to the significant positive changes in the opinions of whites on this subject. Blacks are also more likely than whites to attribute employment, income, and housing inequalities to racial discrimination (forty-four percent of blacks, compared with twenty-one percent of whites) rather than to other factors.[40]

A 1995 issue of *Newsweek* printed on its cover a collage of people with different skin hues.[41] The accompanying article raised the question of how we can discuss black/white relations when there are so many debates about who is and what is black? Although the article is correct in its assertion that the concept of race does lack scientific precision (even scientific significance), we must recognize that the concept has social significance as long as severe disparities in income, education, and occupation still exist between black and white America. In focusing on debates of the semantics of race, we are diverting attention from the more important issue of how blacks can gain the same opportunities afforded to white Americans.

In fact, it is becoming fashionable to be racist in some arenas. The fact that the numerous bombings of black churches during the 1990s were dismissed as acts by a handful of psychopaths perpetuates the myth that African Americans are not under attack by dominant society. Moreover, there is a resurgence of fraternity members dressing in blackface on campuses. At the University of Oklahoma fraternity of Alpha Gamma Rho, a national agricultural fraternity had a recent Halloween party (October 2002) at which members wore Ku Klux Klan robes and blackface. Pictures from this party were posted on the Web. In one picture, a member in blackface wears a prisoner's costume; smiling, he stands sandwiched between two frat brothers—one dressed in a Klan costume and the other clad in overalls and a Confederate flag bandana—as a mock noose dangles above his head. A Halloween party thrown by white fraternities at the University of Virginia (October 2002) included some guests dressing in blackface.

In addition to these egregious acts, three men—two firefighters and a police officer—rode on a racially offensive float in the Broad Channel, Queens Labor Day Parade. The float was entitled "Black to the Future: Broad Channel 2098." The float consisted of a flatbed truck on top of which the men sat with a large bucket of fried chicken and watermelons. The men wore blackface and Afro wigs made of mops, and they mockingly engaged in various civil rights chants, including "No justice, no peace." Bringing the display to a new low, one of the men announced, "Look what they did to our brother in Texas, we would not allow them here . . ." and proceeded to hang by his hands from the back of the truck. In carrying out this stunt, he was manifestly parodying the dragging murder of James Byrd, Jr.—a black man whom three white men killed in Jasper, Texas. To the cheers of spectators, the firefighter repeated his display. Today's racist ideology is certainly prevalent.

In many ways, we are regressing regarding race relations in this country. The research conducted by Paul Ephross and his associates of the National Institute Against Prejudice and Violence suggests that hate crimes are in fact increasing, especially on university campuses across the country.[42] Such public displays of racism suggest that the conditions are such in our society that to be in blackface is okay.

One of among the most recent flagrant obscenities involving racism was made by Mississippian senator and (former) majority leader Trent Lott. During a birthday celebration for South Carolina senator and former presidential candidate Strom Thurmond, who ran on a segregationist platform, Lott toasted: "I want to say this about my state: When Strom Thurmond ran for president, we voted for him. We're proud of it. And if the rest of the country had followed our lead, we wouldn't have had all these problems over all these years, either."[43] Who is the "we" in Lott's declaration? The white people of the South who used the powers of the state and local governments to impose the racial caste system called Jim Crow on their fellow citizens. What were "all these problems" Lott wished to avoid? The triumph of legal equality for African Americans, including, in the south, the long-denied right to vote. The victory was won, despite the hostility of segregationists like Lott and Thurmond, by people of very humble means who struggled valiantly for years, through pain and bloodshed, to overcome the stranglehold of Americans' apartheid.

Lott eventually resigned as Senate majority leader. Nonetheless, on the same day Lott resigned, Republican Congressman Cass Ballenger of North Carolina told the *Charlotte Observer* that Georgia Democratic representative

Cynthia McKinney was "a bitch" whose politics had so provoked him that "I must admit I had segregationist feelings."[44] Like Lott when his approving comments about segregationist Strom Thurmond's 1948 presidential campaign caused a storm of protest, Ballenger insisted that he was guilty only of a poor "choice of words."

Tennessee Senator Bill Frist replaced Trent Lott as Senate majority leader. But a close inspection reveals that Frist's congressional record is no better than Trent Lott's regarding civil rights initiatives: The National Association for the Asvancement of Colored People (NAACP) gives Frist a fifteen percent approval rating in its latest survey of Senate votes compared with twelve percent for Lott;[45] the latest National Hispanic Leadership Agenda survey gave Frist eighteen percent to Lott's twenty-seven.[46] A People for the American Way study of the voting records of Lott, Frist, and the three other contenders for Senate leader (Mitch McConnell, Don Nickles and Rick Santorum) showed that all five cast identical votes on civil rights measures that include the Employment Nondiscrimination Act of 1996 and the Hate Crimes Expansion Act of 2000.[47]

The reason the White House turned on Lott had little to do with distaste for the Mississippian's remarks at Thurmond's 100th birthday party; it moved only when it appeared the controversy might expose a penchant to "play the race card" when convenient. Bush, in trouble in the 2000 primaries, appeared at Bob Jones University, which lost its tax-exempt status for maintaining a policy by which "students who date outside their own race will be expelled." His attorney general, John Ashcroft, led the fight against desegregating Missouri schools and praised Confederate generals as "Southern patriots." Recent evidence of this include the fact that Bush sidestepped Congress earlier this year by directly appointing Mississippi judge, Charles Pickering, who once linked gays with social ills facing America to the federal appeals court by executive ordr even though the nomination was tied up in Congress by a Democratic filibuster. The appointment, bypassing confirmation, is valid until the next Congress takes office in January 2005. There are also concerns about Pickering's handling of a 1994 hate crime incident involving three men who burned an 8-foot cross on the lawn of an interracial family while using racial epithets. The family had been a frequent target of harassment in their small rural town, including having bullets fired into their home and "KKK" painted nearby on the street. When sentencing one of the defendants, Pickering gave what was considered a "lenient" sentence for the cross-burning, in order to "make the punishment commensurate with the drunken prank that I think it was, even though it did have racial overtones."

As the Lott controversy played out, prominent conservatives griped that attention to Republican positioning on race might make it politically unpalatable for the White House to back a challenge to race-based affirmative action in a pending Supreme Court case. And the *Wall Street Journal* condemned Lott's "unprincipled apologies"—particularly his sudden embrace of affirmative action—for steering the Republican Party "away from clear thinking about race."[48] What these conservatives want is a return to the pre-Lott days when it was possible for the President's aides to sell him as a "new kind of Republican" while quietly using race-based appeals.

Republicans are not the only members in Congress who have not supported civil rights initiatives. Initiatives such as those passed under the Clinton Administration, including the Welfare Reform Act, promote a move back to the past and are a blatant attack on the poor and ethnic minorities. Never mind that the foundation of the Administration's arguments is composed of inaccurate information sometimes supported by distortions and negative stereotypes in the media. Politicians use these distortions and stereotypes to present inaccurate information to the public. For example, during his tenure as Speaker of the House, Newt Gingrich, drawing from media's inaccurate depiction of the African American "welfare queen," argued that women on welfare tend to stay there forever. The fact is that fifty percent of recipients exit Aid to Families with Dependent Children (AFDC) in the first year of welfare. Seventy-five percent of recipients exit in the first two years of welfare.[49] Some politicians further maintain that women on welfare have huge families. The truth is that the typical welfare family is made up of a mother and two children, which is a little smaller than the national average for U.S. families.[50] Some members of Congress further maintain that welfare mothers live extravagant lives. The truth is that there is not a single state in which the combined value of AFDC and food stamps lifts a family out of poverty, which was defined as $11,522 per year in 1993 for a family of three. Some politicians imply that only black women are on welfare. The truth is that African American women make up thirty-nine percent of the AFDC rolls, whites thirty-eight percent, Latinas seventeen percent, Asians three percent and Americans Indians one percent. Two percent are of unknown racial origin.[51]

But the strength of the media image continues to influence perceptions. We "know" these things to be true because we have seen them on television, in magazines and in feature films. Knowing this, politicians are certain to reinforce public opinion. President Clinton, in an attempt to exploit the role of media, supported a resolution by Congress to apologize for slavery. House Concurrent Resolution 96 states: "Resolved by the House of Representatives (the Senate concurring), that the Congress apologizes to African Americans whose ancestors suffered as slaves under the Constitution and laws of the United States until 1865."[52] Rather than issue an empty apology, the President and Congress should have supported more initiatives that would have assisted African Americans. President Clinton himself stated that: "Affirmative action has given us a whole generation of professionals in fields that used to be exclusive clubs, where people like me got the benefit of one hundred percent affirmative action."[53] What most people do not realize is that descendants of Africans have spent more time in slavery than being free in this country. And we are dealing with that legacy. Just as white America has benefited from the education, life experiences, and wealth that was handed down to them by their ancestors, so too have African Americans been harmed by the institution of slavery. When anyone speaks out against these inaccuracies, especially when the suggestion is made that this country's history of slavery and continued subjugation are more determinants of the status of African Americans today than laziness, the response tends to be that those things are in the past, and that African Americans are using the "race card" to obtain unfair access to society's resources.

RATIONAL DISCRIMINATION

Similar to the egregious errors embedded in the Herrnstein and Murray study, in *The End of Racism,* Dinesh D'Souza argues that slavery is a natural phenomenon because all past civilizations have had some form of it.[54] D'Souza further maintains that some forms of discrimination are rational. It is a fact, for example, that African Americans are more likely as a group to engage in street crimes than whites. From that, D'Souza proclaims that it is all right for an employer not to hire a highly qualified African American because that employer can rationally consider the applicant's membership in a group with negative characteristics. In D'Souza's own words, "Perhaps discrimination exists because it is rational. It is efficient. It makes economic sense."[55] D'Souza's sophomoric fallacy is germane to the present study. Although rational discrimination is an alluring theory, it is also a theory that is fatally flawed. First, it relies on the idea that race in and of itself determines behavior; second, it assumes race is an unbiased indicator of everything from criminality to employment aptitude; and, finally, it calls for inequality to be institutionalized by law, going against the moral fiber of every American concept of fairness, justice, and individual rights. An analysis of blacks' involvement in crime, a hot-button political topic and a nexus of dominant society's fears, seemingly provides ample evidence of rational discrimination's flaws. D'Souza relies heavily on spicy quotes from black criminals, yet nowhere does the book break down crime statistics by socioeconomic status. To do that would reveal that, at every income level, blacks and whites have similar crime rates; the fact that black America is poorer than white America—not any inherent racial proclivities—underlies the differences in commissions of crime. This breakdown does not even take into consideration race itself, including the fact that African Americans are incarcerated at rates far exceeding their commission of crimes, and receive fifty percent more jail time for committing the same crimes as whites.[56]

Socioeconomic status largely predicts not only crime but education levels, drug use, and even marriage rates because men who do not have steady incomes tend not to marry and form strong families. As discussed earlier, the story of the black underclass begins with the economic privations of slavery and continues with the workforce disadvantage African Americans have faced ever since. Even D'Souza admits that blacks are correct in their frequent assertion that it is a disadvantage to be a young black male today. It is simply logic, not liberalism, not political correctness, to say that a group that begins with disadvantage and remains disadvantaged will be disadvantaged right down to markers of disadvantage, including joblessness, under-education, and crime.

But even if black crime has its roots in socioeconomic status, are not white Americans simply making rational judgments in discriminating against young black males? The answer to this question is the second problem with rational discrimination: the groups in which we find ourselves classified are not, in and of themselves, rational. The Massachusetts Department of Public Health looked at crime and murder rates in various Boston neighborhoods. Southie, which is virtually all white, has the same murder and crime rate as Roxbury, a largely black neighborhood. Both neighborhoods are poor.

In his own neighborhood, a young man from Southie or Roxbury could be seen as an equal criminal risk. Yet, take one from each neighborhood and place him on a street in downtown Boston. Instantly, the man from Southie loses his identification as someone from a criminal context and is free to make his way on his own merits—to be judged as America's ideals of equality demand. The black man from Roxbury, in the same situation, is still defined as a member of an overarching negative group and, according to rational discrimination, will be penalized even if he leads an exemplary life.

The goal of all this rhetoric is to pave the way for an America that legally sanctions discrimination. D'Souza argues for the repeal of the Civil Rights Act, and he makes clear his theory of rational discrimination applies not only to blacks but to "women, who may get pregnant and leave (a job), or to the elderly, who are more likely to fall ill." In this context, rational discrimination is nothing less than institutionalized inequality, the most un-American of civic goals.

Perhaps the best example is, yet again, crime. The horrible rape and murder in 1996 of a woman jogging late at night in New York's Central Park is an example in point. Although a handful of women argue that jogging at late hours makes a political statement about the need for police presence, it is rational to say that women (and men) would be safer if they did not jog in the park after sunset. It is another step entirely to argue that because women are not safe, we should legalize rape and murder in Central Park. In calling for an end to the Civil Rights Act and saying that employers should legally be allowed to discriminate, D'Souza is proposing a racial equivalent to the legalization of crime. But whereas we as a nation should be appalled by this vision, many of us are instead entranced.

Such infatuation could not come at a worse time; America is beginning a new millennium that will see nonwhite citizens become the largest number of citizens in America. Anyone who opposes the concept of a perpetually divided America, separate and unequal, must make their views known now, before rational discrimination proves to be an irrationally beguiling proposition.

During the 1960s and 1970s, critics of mass media suggested that mass media inadvertently assisted in steps toward racial equality. For example, during civil rights protests, police dogs were shown biting little children, fire hoses were used to thump people around like rag dolls and police were shown beating protesters mercilessly. Today, media critics suggest that mass media perpetuates racism at least as much as in its earliest years. Perhaps the turning point was a suit by Allan Bakke in 1974, accusing the University of California Medical School at Davis of reverse discrimination.

The decision handed down by the Supreme Court in the Bakke case was ambiguous; a victory neither for Bakke nor for those opposed to his position. At the heart of the issue was the nation's commitment not only to provide equal opportunities to all citizens today, regardless of color, but also to redress the injustices of the past—injustices that have placed blacks at a considerable disadvantage in the competition for desirable jobs. Through mass media, the term *reverse discrimination* soon made its way into popular discourse. However, a close examination of the concept reveals that it is an oxymoron. This term implies that a subordinate group is discriminating against a dominate group. How can African Americans discriminate against Anglos when Anglos disproportionately own society's resources? An Anglo student once asked in class what would one call an incident in which a white person applies for a job at a black-owned company and is turned down because he or she is white? The answer is discrimination. Realistically, this scenario seldom happens. The American Civil Liberties Union reports that less than two percent of discrimination complaints involve members of dominant society being discriminated against by members of subordinate groups. Yet, if we look at recent publications, popular films, and television programs, we are left with the impression that white males are often discriminated against.

Since Bakke, the courts have been called on again and again to decide whether the nation can legally redress the market effects of past injustices of slavery and discrimination against blacks. Quotas, timetables, and set-asides have all been challenged. For the time being, the tide has shifted against the struggle of blacks for equality as a conservative judiciary, including the Supreme Court, has made numerous decisions that have chipped away at the very foundations of the fight against persistent racial discrimination. In fact, conservatives have successfully challenged affirmative action programs in the university systems of several states, notably California and Texas. Another Supreme Court confrontation drew closer recently when the justices agreed to decide whether the admissions practices at the University of Michigan illegally discriminate against white applicants. The issue should get a thorough airing; on the record will be hundreds of pages of studies on the academic benefits of racial diversity compiled by a Michigan professor. Curt Levey of the Center for Individual Rights, which brought the suit, is hoping for a definitive ruling that could affect not just public universities but every college that accepts federal money, even by way of student loans. Theodore Shaw of the NAACP Legal Defense Fund, which supports affirmative action, gamely asserts that among several similar suits making their way through the courts, this is one of the stronger cases from the defense side. But Shaw, well aware that Bakke was decided by only one vote, by a court that has grown only more conservative since, adds that "if we had our druthers, we wouldn't be here at all."[57]

In 1997, President Bill Clinton called for a national discussion on race. Although the call is a necessary one, it is important to bear in mind that there is already a national conversation about race—it is just that people are having the conversation with people like themselves. Blacks are talking to blacks and whites are talking to whites. Asians are talking to Asians and Latinos are talking to Latinos. Even worse, most people talk about crime and race with few facts. This leads us to continue to exhort the opinions and ideas we already believe to be true. We rarely allow ourselves to entertain new perspectives.

NOTES

1. James M. Washington (Ed.). *A Testament of Hope: The Essential Writings and Speeches of Martin Luther King, Jr.* (San Francisco: Harper Collins, 1986), 580–581.

2. The term "precept" has at least two possible meanings: one as a broad analytical concept, and a second in a more restrictive legal sense. The first, "a command or principle intended as a 'general rule of action,'" denotes the implicit understanding of racial differences. In this context, the inferiority of African Americans was given the standing of a natural principle embodied through the existing moral and social climate of the time that was not to be questioned. In a legal sense, there is the alternative definition of *precept*, as suggested by Ruggero J. Aldisert, which covers three concepts: a rule of law, a legal principle, and a legal doctrine. Used in this manner, the term "precept" encompasses the legal mandates explicitly written in the law and legal orders, which established, legitimized, and enforced the inferior position of African Americans before the law. See, especially, A. Leon Higginbotham Jr. *Shades of Freedom: Racial Politics and Presumptions of the American Legal Process* (New York: Oxford University Press, 1996); and Derrick Bell. *Race, Racism and American Law*, 4th ed. (Gaithersburg, MD: Aspen Law and Business, 2000).

3. Glenn C. Loury. *The Anatomy of Racial Inequality* (Cambridge, MA: Harvard University Press, 2002), 20.

4. Louis Aptheker. *Afro-American History: The Modern Era* (New York: Citadel Press, 1971).

5. Ted Turner was sponsored by the Howard University School of Communication. (October 10, 1995). Washington, DC.

6. The term *minority group* was first suggested by Donald M. Young in *American Minority Peoples* (New York: Harper, 1932), xviii. The definition of *minority group* often used by many sociologists is Louis Wirth's, who defined a minority group as:

a group of people who, because of their physical or cultural characteristics, are singled out from others in the society in which they live for differential and unequal treatment and who therefore regard themselves as objects of collective discrimination.

See, especially, Louis Wirth. "The Problem of Minority Groups," in Ralph Linton (Ed.), *The Science of Man in the World Crisis* (New York: Columbia University Press, 1945), 347.

7. George Simpson and J. Milton Yinger. *Racial and Cultural Minorities: An Analysis of Prejudice and Discrimination*, 5th ed. (New York: Plenum, 1985).

8. Some critics of the majority/minority distinction of racism argue that the terms *majority* and *minority* imply that there is a superior culture for the majority group and an inferior culture for the minority group. That is to say that there is something lacking in the minority culture that makes it inferior. This delineation does not hide the obvious: groups do differ in their aspirations and values, and in ways that may well affect their prospects for mobility. However, the point to be made here is that these cultural differences, when they exist, properly mark the beginning, not the end, of social science inquiry: cultural differences must be explained in terms of their historical and material sources. It is only when culture is taken at face value and

treated as self-explaining that we fall into the trap of imputing cultural superiority to groups on the top and cultural inferiority to groups on the bottom.

9. Examples of this include the discriminatory practices that existed for African Americans around voting in the South: poll taxes and ridiculous literacy tests levied against African Americans so that they would be unable to participate in the political process. As a result, very talented and capable African Americans were excluded from leadership positions in politics. Prisons are yet another example of Graves' first point. Because African Americans are more likely to be arrested and subsequently end up in our criminal justice system, they are least likely to make valuable contributions to society.

10. The correlation between poverty and crime is well documented and unfortunate African Americans and other ethnic minorities are blamed for most of the poverty in the United States as if they invented it. Furthermore, African Americans are more likely to be perceived as responsible for comprising the welfare roles in this country, whereas the real welfare winners are found in big business. Michael Moore, in his controversial book entitled *Downsize This!*, reports the following.

- The United States paid $1.6 million, using federal funds, to McDonald's in part to help them market Chicken McNuggets in Singapore from 1986 to 1994.

- The United States gave $278 million in government technology subsidies to Amoco, AT&T, Citicorp, Du Pont, General Electric, General Motors, and IBM between 1990 and 1994 while, together, they cut 339,038 jobs and posted combined profits of $25.2 billion in 1994 alone.

- Westinghouse was allowed to accelerate the depreciation on their machinery, saving them $215 million in taxes in 1993 while they eliminated 24,700 jobs.

- Exxon was allowed to claim nearly $300 million in tax deductions on the settlement they paid when the Exxon Valdez spilled 11 million gallons of oil into Prince William Sound.

- Pillsbury received $11 million to promote the Pillsbury Dough Boy in foreign countries.

- Royal Caribbean Cruise Lines was allowed a special tax code to pay zero taxes from 1989 to 1992 on a profit of $158 million.

- Forty-two Fortune 500 companies that paid no federal income taxes from 1981 through 1985 until a minimum tax was forced on them in 1986.

Michael Moore. *Downsize This!* (New York: Crown Publishers, 1996), 44–45.

11. The Big Sandy Independent School District in East Texas is located next to the Alabama–Coushatta reservation; as a result, many of the students in the schools are American Indians. In some tribes, it is tradition for males to grow their hair long and cut it only for special ceremonies or rituals such as a funeral, for example. The officials at the Big Sandy Independent School District believed that males should not have long hair and thus demanded that the American Indian boys cut their hair. The boys refused and filed a class action lawsuit against the school district and won. The school district appealed all the way to the Supreme Court, costing the district over $250,000. It is important to point out that the starting salary of teachers in this district is $21,000. This case is an excellent example of how racism requires society to

invest a good deal of time and money to defend the social and institutional barriers that prevent the full participation of all members.

12. In 1948, South Africa was granted its independence from the United Kingdom, and the National Party, dominated by the Afrikaners, assumed control of the government. Under the leadership of this party, the rule of white supremacy, already well under way in the colonial period as custom, become more and more formalized into law. To deal with the multiracial population, the whites devised a policy called apartheid to ensure their dominance. During the 1980s, the organization Trans-Africa under the leadership of Randall Robinson, spearheaded the movement to influence U.S. policies toward Africa and the Caribbean and, as a result, South Africa became isolated both politically and socially.

13. Derrick Bell reminds us that:

What appears to be progress toward racial justice is, in fact, a cyclical process. Barriers are lowered in one era only to reveal a new set of often more sophisticated but no less effective policies that maintain blacks in a subordinate status. Their status as slaves from the seventeenth through much of the nineteenth centuries evolved into segregation after a brief Reconstruction period. And the post-Brown period in the mid-twentieth century has brought us the "eerily awful equal opportunity era": "eerie" because some blacks seem to be making substantial moves into the mainstream; "awful" because so many blacks have disappeared into poverty with all its afflictions.

Derrick Bell, *Race, Racism and American Law*, 27.

14. The arrest of suspect Rodney King by the Los Angeles police was caught on videotape that revealed six officers wielding their batons at a defenseless King. At trial the officers defended their actions, claiming that the law allows them as much force as necessary to subdue an arrestee and that King was resisting. All six of the officers were exonerated. This outcome sparked one of the worst riots in contemporary history. The rioters felt a great disrespect for the law because they believed that the law did not protect or apply to them. These illustrations of how racism and discrimination lead to a dysfunctional society are adapted from Richard Schaefer. *Racial and Ethnic Groups*, 9th ed. (Upper Saddle River, NJ: Prentice Hall, 2002); and, Joseph Graves, *The Emperor's New Clothes*, 2001.

15. See, especially, John Hope Franklin. *From Slavery to Freedom* (New York: Knopf, 1947).

16. Orlando Patterson notes:

There is nothing notably peculiar about the institution of slavery. It has existed from before the dawn of human history right down to the twentieth century, in the most primitive of human societies and in the most civilized. There is no region on earth that has not at some time harbored the institution. Probably there is no group of people whose ancestors were not at one time slaves or slaveholders.

Orlando Patterson. *Slavery and Social Death: A Comparative Study* (Cambridge: Harvard University Press, 1982), vii.

17. See, especially, Lerone Bennett. *Before the Mayflower: A History of Black America* (New York: Penguin Books, 1984).

18. Bart Landry. "The Enduring Dilemma of Race in America," in Alan Wolfe (Ed.), *America At Century's End* (Los Angeles: University of California Press, 1991), 185–207.

19. Higginbotham, *Shades of Freedom*, 13.

20. Higginbotham, 14; Bell, *Race, Racism and American Law*, 2.

21. Samuel Cartwright. "The Prognathous Species of Mankind," in Eric L. McKitrick (Ed.), *Slavery Defended* (Englewood Cliffs, NJ: Prentice Hall, 1963), 139–147.

22. Lewis Carlson and George Colburn, (Eds.). *In Their Place* (New York: John Wiley, 1972).

23. Ibid.

24. See, especially, I. Newby. *Jim Crow's Defense* (Baton Rouge: Louisiana State University Press, 1965).

25. Graves, *The Emperor's New Clothes*, 2.

26. Eugenia Shanklin. *Anthropology and Race* (Belmont, CA: Wadsworth, 1994).

27. Leonard Lieberman, Blaine W. Stevenson and Larry T. Reynolds. "Race and Anthropology: A Core Concept Without Consensus," *Anthropology and Education Quarterly* 20 (1989): 7–73.

28. Richard Lewontin. "The Fallacy of Biological Determinism," in David E. Hunter and Phillip Whitten, (Eds.), *Readings in Physical Anthropology and Archaeology* (New York: Harper and Row, 1978): 79–94.

29. F. Marks. *Human Bio-diversity* (New York: Walter de Gruyter, 1995).

30. Alice N. Brues. "The Objective View of Race," *Napa Bulleting* 13 (1993): 74–78. This habit of sorting the world's peoples into a small number of groups got its first scientific gloss from Swedish taxonomist Carolus Linnaeus. Linnaeus is best known for his system of classifying living things by genus and species—Escherichia coli, Homo sapiens, and the rest. In 1758, he declared that humanity falls into four races: white (Europeans), red (Native Americans), dark (Asians), and black (Africans). Linnaeus said that Native Americans (who in the 1940s got grouped with Asians) were ruled by custom. Africans were indolent and negligent, and Europeans were inventive and gentle. Leave aside the racist undertones, not to mention the oddity of ascribing gentleness to the group that perpetrated the Crusades and Inquisition; astonishing enough is that the notion and the specifics of race predate genetics, evolutionary biology, and the science of human origins. With the revolutions in those fields, how is it that the eighteenth century scheme of race retains its powerful hold?

31. National Center for Health Statistics, United States Health 1994, pp. 210. Available at http://www.edc.gov/nchs/products/pubs/hus/tables/2002/02hus068.pdf. See, also, Ellis Cose. *The Rage of a Privileged Class* (New York: Perennial, 1995).

32. The television news magazine *20/20* aired a segment (spring, 1992) entitled "An Experiment in Race." Two young males, one white, one African American, were monitored in St. Louis at department stores, apartment rental offices, car lots, and a

job agency. Both men were considered to be middle class and dressed similarly. The African American male was followed in one department store and then completely ignored in another, whereas in the same store, with the same salesman, the white male was given immediate attention and treated warmly. When they went to inquire about housing at an apartment rental agency, the white male was given keys to inspect several apartments and was told that there were apartments available for immediate occupancy—the African American male was told by the same agent that there were no available apartments and that he had just rented the last one that same morning. When inquiring about jobs at a job placement agency, the white male was given a list of jobs and strongly encouraged by the agent to apply, whereas the same agent lectured the African American male about laziness and arriving to work on time. In all of the incidents, the African American male was blatantly discriminated against.

33. Joe Feagin and Clairece Booher Feagin. *Racial and Ethnic Relations*, 4th ed. (Englewood Cliffs, NJ: Prentice Hall, 1993), 214.

34. Richard Herrnstein and Charles Murray. *The Bell Curve: Intelligence and Class Structure in America* (New York: The Free Press, 1994).

35. Ibid.

36. Michael Hout, Samuel Lucas, and Kim Voss. *Inequality by Design: Cracking the Bell Curve Myth* (Princeton, NJ: Princeton University Press, 1996).

37. Ibid., Hout, Lucas, and Voss, *Inequality by Design*, 6.

38. In 1980, when they were fifteen to twenty-three years old, the participants took the Armed Forces Qualifying Test.

39. Gallup Poll News Service, July 1997.

40. Gallup Poll News Service, January 1994.

41. *Newsweek* (13 February 1995).

42. Paul H. Ephross, Arnold Barnes, Howard J. Ehrlich, Kathleen R. Sandnes, and Joan C. Weiss. *The Ethnoviolence Project: Pilot Study* (Baltimore, MD: National Institute Against Prejudice and Violence, 1986). More recently, an Indiana University student, Benjamin Smith, gunned down Won-Joon Yoon, an Indiana University graduate student, as Yoon was leaving a Christian Korean church in Bloomington, Indiana. Smith's motivation was that he wanted to rid the world of nonwhites and gays.

43. John Meacham, "A Man Out of Time," *Newsweek* (23 December 2002), 28.

44. Associated Press, *New York Times,* 21 December 2002, p. 18.

45. Reggie Beehner, "Lott Among Lowest-Scoring Senators in Voting for Minority Issues," *Sun Herald*, 19 December 2002.

46. Patty Reinert, "Lott Gaffe Angers Latinos; Soft GOP Reaction Shakes Fragile Hispanic Support," *Houston Chronicle*, 2002, p. 16.

47. As reported by Tavis Smiley. "Ralph Neas, People for the American Way, and Paul Rosenzweig, The Heritage Foundation, Discuss the Bush Administration's Policies on Race," National Public Radio, 19 December 2002.

48. As reported on *The Chris Matthews Show*, 15 December 2002; NBC; various times. Guests included Clarence Page, *Chicago Tribune*; Peggy Noonan, *Wall Street*

Journal; and David Gregory of NBC. Topic: "This Week's Remarks and Apologies by Senator Trent Lott."

49. Congressional Research Service and Human Health Services, Administration for Children and Families, 2001. United States Census Bureau, 2001.

50. Ibid., Congressional Research Service, 5.

51. Ibid., 1–4.

52. As quoted in George E. Curry, "A Better Way to Apologize," *Emerge* (January 1998), editor's note.

53. Curry, "A Better Way to Apologize," editor's note.

54. Dinesh D'Souza. *The End of Racism* (New York: Free Press), 245–287.

55. D'Souza, *The End of Racism*, 59

56. See, especially, Marc Mauer. "A Generation Behind Bars: Black Males and the Criminal Justice System," in Richard G. Majors and Jacob U. Gordon (Eds.), *The American Black Male: His Present Status and His Future* (Chicago: Nelson-Hall Publishers, 1994), 8.

57. Jerry Adler, "Affirmative Action: Back to the Supremes," *Newsweek* (16 December 2002), 8.

3

Theory: UCR, Racial Bias, Public Policy, and the Mass Media

The image of violent white Americans as social bandits was carried well into the post–World War II era. It appealed, of course, primarily to young white males. "Almost every boy in America," wrote one criminologist, "wanted to be Jesse James, the strong, fearless bandit who came to symbolize the individuality of the American West." This image effectively "white-washed" the seriousness of white violence in the American consciousness through a process of turning attention away from the blood and horror of white predatory crime and refocusing it on fabricated, overly romanticized biographies. Whereas black violence was seen as dark and threatening, there was something quintessentially American about violence when it was rendered by whites. Diminished in its importance, violence then became an accepted and altogether normal rite of passage for millions of American white youths. . . . The group that defines the law and controls public opinion is the group that will define criminal images and control the punishments for all groups, not the least of which will be their own. Throughout history, white Americans have done precisely that. Through law and culture, they have created a condition whereby white American violence has become imageless. Yet when viewed in the broad scope of history, they do have an image, a very clearly defined image. From the landing of the Vikings to the present day, white American males have used their dominant social status to exercise habitual cruelty against weaker and less powerful people. There is only one word for that. Alas, the predatory white criminal is nothing less than a bully.[1]

In the Watergate scandal, twenty-one of Nixon's aides were sent to prison for their crimes. G. Gordon Liddy, who was uncooperative with investigators, served fifty-two months. The others served prison terms ranging from four to twelve months. Nixon himself received a pardon.

Nine years after Nixon's resignation, Frank Willis—the security guard who discovered the Watergate break-in—was arrested for shoplifting in Augusta, Georgia. Unemployed at the time, he had stolen a pair of shoes for his son. Unlike "the president's men," Mr. Willis received the maximum sentence: twelve months in prison for stealing a $12 pair of shoes.[2]

The window into crime that is gazed through by mass media is usually "street crime" that is obtained from police reports and other sources used to compile the Uniform Crime Reports (UCR). Since 1930, the U.S. Department of Justice has compiled national crime statistics, the UCR, with the Federal Bureau of Investigation (FBI) assuming responsibility as the clearinghouse and publisher. Although participation in the UCR program by local police departments is purely voluntary, the comprehensiveness of the information has steadily improved over the years, with police departments from large metropolitan areas historically being the best participants.[3]

Historically, the UCR has been divided into two parts. Part I crimes consist of the Index Crimes, major felonies that are believed to be serious, to occur frequently, and to have a greater likelihood of being reported to the police. These felonies include murder, rape, robbery, burglary, and motor theft, for example. Part II offenses include fraud, embezzlement, forgery and counterfeiting, and runaways, for example.

It is important to realize from the start that the Crime Index is not a priori blind to race. This does not suggest that the Crime Index is necessarily biased by conscious social intent; rather, it is biased by everyday social life. This view is based on an understanding of race-related opportunities in contemporary America. The present Uniform Crime Reports Index (UCR) lists street crime and excludes white-collar and probably most middle-class–related crimes. Because African Americans are underrepresented and whites overrepresented in white-collar occupations, the set of crimes called Index Crimes is therefore skewed away from criminal opportunities in which whites are overrepresented. This does not imply that the Crime Index is biased against lower-class black street crime per se, but rather that it is biased away from middle-class and elite whites' "suite" crimes. This type of crime includes such crimes as stock market fraud, price-fixing and product misrepresentation, corporate tax evasion, industrial pollution, maintenance of unsafe working conditions, and illegal intervention in the political process.

Because race is strongly correlated with the occupancy of white-collar positions, and because the conventional UCR Crime Index is intrinsically biased away from white-collar crime, the UCR Crime Index plainly is intrinsically biased away from the arrest of mostly white-collar criminals and toward blacks and blue-collar offenders.[4] Thus, the public's beliefs about crime, such as what types of people are more likely to commit crime, where crime is most likely to occur, and who is most likely to become a victim is directly related to the social construction of crime. For example, consider how poor and rich communities are policed and the social origins of crime to explain the differences in criminal behavior among groups. Police have wide latitude in deciding when to enforce laws and make arrests. Their decision is greatest when dealing with minor offenses, such as disorderly conduct. Sociological research has shown that police discretion is strongly influenced by class and race judgments. The police are more likely to arrest persons they perceive as troublemakers, and they are more likely to make arrests when the complainant is white. They are less likely to arrest middle-class, white, and prominent citizens.[5] In addition, minority communities are policed much more intensively, which leads to more frequent arrests of those who live there.

In addition, a recent report on juvenile offenders demonstrates that black and Latino youths with no prior record of crime are treated far more severely in the juvenile-justice system than whites, also with no prior criminal record, of comparable social class. Minority youths are more likely to be arrested, held in jail, sent to juvenile or adult court for trial, convicted, and given longer prison terms. The racial disparities in the juvenile-court system are magnified with each additional step into the justice system. In some cases, the racial disparities are stunning. For example, the report notes that although twenty-five percent of arrested white youths are sent to adult prison, nearly sixty percent of arrested black youths are. That is truly a wide racial disparity. The report concludes that these racial disparities lie not so much in overt discrimination on the part of prosecutors, judges, and other court personnel, but instead in the stereotypes that these decision makers rely on at each point of the juvenile-justice system. Being black, wearing low-hung, baggy pants, and sporting dreadlocks is likely to get a person quickly through the various stages of the juvenile-justice system and into prison. The report concludes that race, as distinct from the effect of social class, is "undeniably" a major factor in the dispensation of juvenile justice.[6]

THE CREATION OF THE BLACK DEMON STEREOTYPE

The crime, as the tearful young mother reported it, was demonic: a carjacking in which a thief roared off with her two infants still inside. The mother's wrenching pleas for the safe return of her sons were made to the national media, which had gathered in the small city of Union, South Carolina, to report the story's outcome in all its pathos. Much of the nation was transfixed by the pictures of the angelic infants and by Susan Smith's mask of grieving motherhood. Looming as a backdrop to these images of innocence was Smith's description of the demonic figure: an African American male in a skullcap—thus, the nation's portrait of a criminal and a black devil.

But the nation soon discovered that there was no black devil. Smith, the young white mother with the tear-streaked face, possessed by demons of her own, later confessed to authorities that she had strapped her sons into the car and plunged them to their deaths in a nearby lake. But until the moment of truth when the local police officials finally bluffed a confession out of her, there was that image—loose again on the surface of the national consciousness—coming out of the warped mind of antebellum America, out of Thomas Dixon's 1905 novel *The Clansman* and D. W. Griffith's 1915 film *Birth of a Nation*.[7]

Stereotypes have been used historically by some members of dominant society to maintain its control and subjugation of African Americans and other ethnic minorities. Given this pattern of behavior, it should be no surprise then, that African Americans are often depicted as criminals in mass media. Crime in America is often portrayed in blackface, seemingly suggesting not only that African Americans are likely to be involved in crime, but that they are responsible for most of the crime in America today. African Americans are almost always depicted as criminals in mass media, hence illustrating the "black demon" stereotype. To successfully subjugate and exploit a group, negative stereotypes become tools of ideological formation that operate, in part, to suggest that the subordinate group is deserving of such treatment or status. In this section, the theoretical underpinnings of how the black demon stereotype is used by dominant society as a tool to maintain its power over African Americans will be discussed. Germane to this discussion is the origin of the myth of the black rapist, specifically, how this myth is used to justify covert and overt racism. Just as Frederick Douglass argued during the 1850s that the "myth of the black rapist" was created to legitimize lynchings,[8] the criminal image of the black male today is being continuously used to perpetuate dominant society's continued fear and subjugation of African Americans.

THE MYTH OF THE BLACK MALE RAPIST

In the previous chapter, I discussed some of the most egregious effects of the peculiar institution of slavery on black Americans. The institution of lynching is of interest to the present study because it was for many decades an awesome destructive power, murderous to some, menacing to a great many, a constant source of intimidation to all black Southerners young and old, and a daily reminder of their defenselessness. Hence, it is not possible for white America to really understand blacks' distrust of the legal system, or their fears of racial profiling and the police, without understanding how disposable a black life was for so long a time in our nation's history.

Discerning who and what type of person took part in lynchings is made difficult by the fact that those who carried out extralegal punishments were pointedly anonymous. This was both practical—it protected lynchers from arrest and prosecution—and symbolic, in that the lynching was seen as a conservative act, a defense of the status quo. The coroner's inevitable verdict, "Death at the hands of persons unknown," affirmed the public's tacit complicity; no *persons* had committed a crime, because the lynching had been an expression of the community's will. Other protective euphemisms came into play. Lynchers, never identified by name, were "determined men," members of "Judge Lynch's Court," or men "agitated to a high degree;" and eyewitnesses, even law officers, invariably swore they hadn't recognized any of the mob's individual members.[9]

Although the most sensational and commonly repeated excuse for a lynching was a sexual assault by a black man against a white woman, the instigating reasons were actually wide-ranging. The black-owned *Richmond Planet* kept a running tabulation in a column entitled "The Reign of Lawlessness."[10] Where possible, the paper gave the white accusation against the victim that led to the lynchings. In 1897, with two or three lynchings making news every week and a total of 123 black victims recorded for the year, the causes of the incidents ranged from murder, rape, and assault to wanting to have a drink of water and sassing a white lady. In a typical four-week period beginning June 14, 1897, Mrs. Jake Cebrose of Plano, Texas, was lynched for "nothing"; four men accused of murder—Solomon Jackson, Lewis Speir, Jesse Thompson, and Camp Reese—were lynched together in Wetumpka, Alabama; an eight-year-old black child identified only as "Parks" was lynched in South Carolina for "nothing"; Charlie Washington was lynched for "rape and robbery" in Alabama; William Street was burned at the stake for "assault" in Devline, Louisiana; Dan Ogg was put to death in Palestine, Texas, because he was "found in a white family's room"; and Alex Walker of Pleasant Hill, Alabama, had his life snuffed out for "being troublesome."[11] The National Association for the Advancement of Colored People (NAACP), working in the 1930s to combat the southern argument that black men posed an inordinate sexual threat to white women, reviewed its own extensive case files for the actual causes of lynchings over several decades and produced a list that included such infractions as window peeping, making moonshine liquor, slapping a child, conjuring, stealing hogs, not turning out of the road for a white boy in an automobile, and disobeying ferry regulations.

Ida B. Wells was a journalist who was the nation's preeminent antilynching crusader who wrote many articles about the evils of lynchings. In her articles, she addressed how, in the majority of cases, the charge of rape was untrue, and had either been added to a complaint about a black suspect to incense local whites or, in some instances, to obscure the fact that the black man's real sin had been to have consensual sex with a white woman.[12] W. E. B. Du Bois, in his own informal study of the subject, had found that despite the generally held tenet that black men were lynched for assaults on white women, in only twenty-five percent of lynchings was that crime even alleged.[13]

Hence, underlying the growing concerns of people such as Ida B. Wells and W. E. B. Du Bois was their sense that whites were determined to undermine black advances made during Reconstruction and maintain a strict racial caste system in the South at all costs. As Wells had pointed out in one of her columns, the old acquiescent Negro of slave days had been supplanted by his more assertive descendants, and whites, out of fear, had sought new ways to maintain their hegemony. Jim Crow laws, governing virtually every aspect of black people's lives, were instituted while lynching increasingly was directed at those who posed a social, not just a political, threat. Most sensationally, lynching came to be associated with what was seen as the ultimate symbol of black autonomy, sexual access by black men to white women. Beyond this could only lie the nightmare of interbreeding and the blurring of caste lines. And because the idea of such an act drove Southern whites into frenzy, the resulting punishments took on new, perverse forms of cruelty—the tortures and immolations of the spectacle lynching.[14]

Wells was one of the first people in America to perceive that the talk of chivalry and beastlike blacks ravishing white girls was largely fallacious, and that such ideas were being used to help maintain a permanent hysteria to legitimize lynching because it reinforced the notion that the races must be kept separate at all costs. What was particularly insidious about this mythology was that by using as taboo a subject as interracial sex and as ubiquitous a fear as "race pollution," it tended to push more moderate whites, even if they disapproved of lynching, to accept it as necessary.[15]

Wells' personal investigations of lynchings convinced her that almost invariably the charge of rape concealed a more complex truth. The most egregious example Wells found was in Indianola, Mississippi, where, according to a newspaper report, a "big burly brute was lynched because he had raped the seven-year-old daughter of the sheriff." Wells traveled to Indianola and met the alleged rape victim, who was no girl but a grown woman in her late teens. The "brute," Wells learned, had worked on the sheriff's farm for a number of years and was acquainted with every member of the family. The woman had been found in her lover's cabin by her father, who led a lynch mob to save his daughter's reputation. In late May 1892, Wells wrote in the *Free Speech*:

Nobody in this section believes the old thread-bare lie that Negro men assault white women. If Southern white men are not careful they will over-reach themselves and a conclusion will be reached which will be very damaging to the moral reputation of their women.[16]

In her booklet, *Free Speech*, Wells continued to summarize the statistics she had assembled, lamented the gross injustice of lynching and, as in her *Free Speech* articles, scolded the South for its pretense of virtue:

The miscegenation laws of the South only operate against the legitimate union of the races; they leave the white man free to seduce all the colored girls he can, but it is death to the colored man who yields to the force and advances of a similar attraction in white women. . . . It is certain that lynching mobs have not only refused to give the Negro a chance to defend himself, but have killed their victim with a full knowledge that the relationship of the alleged assailant with the woman who accused him, was voluntary and clandestine.[17]

To support her claim, Wells gave examples that exposed the ideal of the pure, virginal southern woman as myth. She mentioned white women running away with their black coachmen; a white woman caught living with a black man who, when arrested for the offense, sought to protect her lover by claiming she herself was black; a white girl who, discovered by her family to be having sex with a mulatto, stole her father's money and ran away with her lover; a white woman who, discovered with her black lover in her bedroom, ingeniously stopped a lynch mob by explaining that she had hired him to hang the curtains. In Natchez, Wells reported, a woman of means who was having secret relations with a black servant gave birth to a child who seemed abnormally dark, but the child's complexion was "traced to some brunette ancestor." Soon another dark child was born to this same woman. Her family suggested all kinds of "medical" explanations including "insufficient air in the womb." A physician, however, called in to clear up the mystery, stunned her loved ones with the announcement that the child was a Negro. The servant, it was discovered, had just left town, headed west.[18]

Wells also took issue with the claim that blacks had of late developed a bestial sexual appetite, a calumny she declared "a falsehood of the deepest dye." If this was so, she asked, why did it not express itself before and during the Civil War, when white Southern men confidently left their women home alone with the slaves, or in Reconstruction, when hundreds of white "Oberlin girls" came to the South to work as teachers in the most heavily black districts?[19]

Wells went further to argue that southern whites, in their belief that black men were preoccupied with having sexual intercourse with white women, were largely battling a monster of their own creation: the long-standing sexual access to black women that white men had enjoyed. To rationalize their continual subjugation of black women in slavery and their use of them as mammies and concubines, white men had come to believe in the fanciful idea that black women were highly sexed animals who encouraged, even welcomed, their own violation. In contrast, influenced by romantic ideals and perhaps to adjust somehow for their animalistic lusting after black women, whites had placed their own women on a pedestal of virtue and purity—the polar opposite of the regard in which black women were held. "Exquisite, fine, beautiful; a creature of peach blossoms and snow, languid, delicate, saucy; now imperious, now melting, always bewitching" was the description of the Southern white woman.

Some prominent examples of how the myth played out include the case of Will Brown, a black man who lived in Omaha, Nebraska. Will Brown was lynched, shot and burned at the stake because he was accused of raping a 19-year-old woman who was white. Brown's guilt, however, was not established by authorities, who considered Brown, about sixty yeras old and crippled with rheumatoid arthritis, physically incapable of the crime. Another case, perhaps better known, is that of the Scottsboro boys. In 1931, Victoria Price and Ruby Bates, two young white women, alleged that they had been assaulted and raped by nine "negro boys." After swift pretrial procedures, eight of the black boys were sentenced to death. The final case resulted in a hung jury. The press portrayed Price and Bates as symbols of Southern white womanhood. Eventually, Bates recanted her story. Another well-documented case involves the 1923 Rosewood, Florida, massacre. A false claim by a white woman that she was raped by a black man led whites in an adjoining town to go on a killing rampage and to burn down the all-black Rosewood. According to official estimates, six blacks and two whites were killed. Unofficial estimates are that between 40 and 150 blacks were killed. More than seventy years later, a court awarded Rosewood family descendants more than 2 million dollars.

In this way, the black demon stereotype was created, especially regarding the inaccurate notion that African American males have a very high propensity toward wanting to rape white women. It is important to point out that although rape is a form of violence, it differs in the cultural imagination significantly from forms of violence that are not committed specifically against women. Moreover, the myth that African American men are particularly prone to raping white women was an especially important part of the mythology that sustained the reign of Jim Crow.[20] It is no accident that lynchings used to enforce white dominance were often based on the allegation that the victim of the lynching had raped a white woman, nor is it coincidence that many of the men on death row in the southern states at that time were African Americans convicted of raping white women.[21] The images and subsequent beliefs caused by this travesty of justice created an image in the minds of many Americans that African American men are violent brutes who could not be trusted, hence the creation of the black demon.

One way in which the labeling of the black demon manifests itself today is discussed in *The Color of Crime: Racial Hoaxes, White Fear, Black Protectionism, Police Harassment, and other Macroaggressions*, a seminal work by Katheryn Russell who documented sixty-seven contemporary cases involving "racial hoaxes" (from 1987 and 1996). Russell defines racial hoaxes as "when someone fabricates a crime and blames it on another person because of his race OR when an actual crime has been committed and the perpetrator falsely blames someone because of his race."[22] Russell's cases involving false accusations of rape include:

- A student at a major East Coast university reported that another white female student had been raped by two young black men with "particularly bad body odor." The accusing student later admitted she had made up the story to "highlight the problems of safety for women."
- A young white lady claimed she had been kidnapped, at gunpoint, from a shopping mall by three black men. She told law enforcement officers that she had been driven around in her car for ten hours, forced to take drugs, and then raped. Police later determined that the woman made up the story so that her parents would not be angry at her for staying out all night.

- A young white girl from Virginia told police that a black man had broken into her family's home and attempted to rape her. The alleged attacker was arrested, charged, and convicted of burglary and attempted rape, and was sentenced to a twelve-year prison term. He was released after fifteen months when the girl recanted her testimony.

- A young white woman told police that she was attacked by a muscular black man who wielded a gun and a knife. DNA evidence was used to show that the woman had made up the entire story.

- A white man in Georgia was brutally murdered and his wife told police that she and her husband had been kidnapped by two black men. The men killed her husband and tried to rape her, she maintained. It was believed that this couple was targeted by blacks because they were Ku Klux Klan (KKK) members. Later, it was discovered that the "grieving widow" actually had a lover who was also a Klansman and he eventually confessed to police that he and the "grieving widow" had killed her husband. Their hopes were to cash in on the insurance policy of the deceased husband.

- A white Florida woman claimed she had been raped and robbed by two black men; a white woman in Baton Rouge told police that she had been sexually assaulted by a black man. Later, she admitted to making up the story.

- A 7-year-old white girl told police she had been assaulted by a black man. After initiating a statewide search for the assailant, the police discovered that the girl had made up the crime.

- A young white woman reported that she and her 71-year-old mother-in-law had been attacked by a black male intruder. The police investigation revealed that the woman had been in a fight with another woman and had come up with the story as a cover-up.

- A white woman in Madison, Wisconsin, told police that a black man snatched her off the sidewalk and raped her. She later admitted that the story was a fabrication. She was not charged with filing a false report.[23]

It is fortunate that two pivotal events have taken place to spotlight the false accusations lodged against African American males: the Oakland Police Corruption Case and Governor George Ryan's (R-Illinois) moratorium on executions. According to the Associated Press, three former Oakland police officers systematically set up young black men and conjured false accusations against them to feed their egos.[24] Clarence "Chuck" Mabanag, Jude Siapno, and Matthew Hornug wanted to increase their arrest numbers. They found it easy to work on their own, and to gather in force to jump out of their vehicle and grab somebody, especially if the person were African American. The scandal, which has resulted in the dismissal of about ninety criminal cases, mostly drug related, and the initiation of seventeen civil-rights suits by 115 people, surfaced after Keith Batt, then a twenty-year-old rookie, reported what he saw on duty with Mabanag, his training officer. Batt painted a disturbing picture of the officers' "stop-and-grab" tactics in which suspects randomly were accosted on the street, handcuffed and put in the patrol car before they were questioned about their activities. The rogue officers believed blacks to be the perfect victims because, Batt quoted, they are inarticulate, uneducated, and defenseless.

Governor Ryan of Illinois, whose state has had a bad record of sentencing innocent people to death, declared a moratorium on executions a few years back. Now, in his final months in office, he is considering commuting the sentences of everyone on death row. His willingness to do so may have been tested last month by televised hearings that underscored the horror of the crimes for which these inmates were sentenced. But despite the bad publicity, Governor Ryan may still commute all the sentences to life in prison.

Illinois has been at the center of the death penalty debate since it was revealed, through DNA evidence, that thirteen of the people sent to its death row since capital punishment was restored in 1977 had been wrongly convicted. That's more than the twelve people who were actually executed. The cochairman of a blue-ribbon commission appointed to study the system noted that it was unlikely that any doctor "could get it wrong over 50 percent of the time and still stay in business."[25] In one case, a convicted murderer who had spent sixteen years on death row was exonerated just two days before his scheduled execution. The investigations into the Illinois exonerations have made it clear how a person who is innocent of a capital crime could nevertheless wind up on death row. Witnesses, from jailhouse snitches to police officers, have testified falsely. Prosecutors, whether out of incompetence or questionable motives, have ignored evidence that these witnesses were often not qualified to testify, or failed to conduct investigations that could have cleared their clients.

A REVISIT OF RICHARD QUINNEY'S SOCIAL REALITY OF CRIME

Why it is that such racial-hoax travesties of justice as the ones presented are allowed to occur? Criminologist Richard Quinney maintains that conflict is intertwined with power—more specifically, because differential distribution of power leads to conflict, conflict is rooted in the competition for power. Quinney's beliefs about power and crime are central to his social reality of crime theory. For Quinney, crime is directly related to people's perceptions of crime; people's perceptions of crime are controlled by persons in powerful positions. As well, the criminal-justice system works to secure and protect the needs of the powerful. When people develop behavior patterns that conflict with these needs, the agents of the rich, the justice system, defines them as criminals.[26] Quinney's theory contains six propositions:

1. *Definition of Crime*: Crime is a definition of human conduct that is created by authorized agents in a politically organized society.

2. *Formulation of Criminal Definitions*: Criminal definitions describe behaviors that conflict with the interests of the segments of society that have the power to shape public policy.

3. *Application of Criminal Definitions*: Criminal definitions are applied by the segments of society that have the power to shape the enforcement and administration of criminal law.

4. *Development of Behavior Patterns in Relation to Criminal Definitions*: Behavior patterns are structured in segmentally organized society in relation to criminal definitions and, within this context, persons engage in actions that have relative probabilities of being defined as criminal.

5. *Construction of Criminal Definitions*: Conceptions of crime are constructed and diffused in the segments of society by various means of communication.

6. *The Social Reality of Crime*: The social reality of crime is constructed by the formulation and application of criminal definitions, the development of behavior patterns to criminal definitions, and the construction of criminal conceptions.[27]

Crime is created, then, because conceptions of crime are constructed and disseminated in the segments of society by various means of communication. Drawing from the work of Peter Berger and Thomas Luckmann,[28] Quinney maintains that what we know as the "real world" is a social construction. Social reality is thus, according to Quinney, the world a group of people create and believe in as their own. This reality is constructed according to the kind of knowledge they develop, the ideas they are exposed to, the manner in which they select information to fit the world they are shaping, and the manner in which they interpret these conceptions.

Moreover, Quinney suggests that among the constructions that develop in a society are those that determine what people regard as crime. Wherever we find the concept of crime, we will find conceptions about the relevance of crime, the offender's characteristics, and the relation of crime to the social order. These constructions are developed through communication. In fact, "the construction of criminal conceptions depends on the portrayal of crime in all personal and mass" communications.[29] By such means, criminal conceptions are constructed and diffused in the segments of society. The most critical conceptions are those held by the power segments of society. These are the conceptions that are likely to become incorporated into the social reality of crime.

In fact, research has shown that crime coverage in the newspaper, television, and movies affect our estimate about the frequency of crime as well as the interpretations we attach to a particular crime,[30] and research has also shown that newspapers present a very unique reality.[31]

Quinney's theory suggests a relationship between the media (particularly television and newspaper), and public-opinion formation. Thus, the rationale for investigating the media's impact on public opinion lies in the fact that the public uses information appearing in the media for the formation of opinions about and perceptions of a given social phenomenon. Because the majority of people have little direct experience with serious crime, especially its causes, it seems reasonable to assume that public perceptions of crime are, to some extent, formed on the basis of information received from the media.

Quinney asserts that it is conceivable that one might find a higher rate of biased crime reports for members of social groups that are perceived as threatening the existing social order. He argues:

The media presentation about crime, whether as fiction or reality, is ultimately based on a general acceptance of the prevailing social and economic order. And so such a basis, the portrayals of crime and crime-fighting inevitably adhere to the legal system and the need to control crime. Crime as we see it in the media is a threat to the American way of life, and the State's right to intervene in controlling crime is presented as the only legitimate reality. This is the ideology presented by officials when they appear in the media and this is the message in the fictional accounts of crime and the law. The ideology and the reality they communicate maintain the established order.[32]

Hence, among the most important agents in disseminating the conceptions of crime are the media of mass communication. Crime coverage in the newspapers, television, and movies affects our estimate about frequency of crime as well as the interpretations we attach to crime.

CONCEPTUAL ENTRAPMENT BY MEDIA IMAGERY

One thing that struck me as I listened to CNN's breathless, all-sniper-all-the-time commentary was the prevalence of precisely such romanticized cowboy vocabulary. Before the arrests, most experts assumed there was a single sniper, most probably "a lone Caucasian man" in his 20s or 30s, someone very "smart," very "calculating," very "cool," "precise," and "controlled." We heard hypotheses about the "pleasure" he was getting from the shootings, the "game" he was playing, the "mysterious," even "superhuman" dimension of his escape artistry and the probability that he had done time with some "elite" branch of the military. It was chilling, all right, but it was also romantic. One could almost envision Bruce Willis in the role.

This script was disrupted right after the arrests, however, when "one Caucasian man" was transmogrified into "a pair of African American males." CNN devoted long hours to revisionist discussions of how "dumb" the suspects had been, about how many clues they'd left, about how "stupid" they were for phoning police, how "idiotic" for demanding money. It was a very polite version of the rampaging-savage narrative, one that doesn't glorify dark culprits, but one that was still undergirded by the perceived social necessity of "good" lone rangers and their well-stocked gun racks as the last bastion of decency, home and hearth.[33]

In chapter 1, I explained what Katheryn Russell meant by "entrapment by media imagery" and listed examples of racial hoaxes.[34] By employing Russell's phrase and drawing from the works of Peter Berger, Thomas Luckmann, and Richard Quinney, I will introduce a schema that will illustrate how the African American male criminal stereotype is created in people's minds and subsequently becomes their definition of crime—the world of crime they believe exists based on their individual knowledge and the knowledge gained from social interactions with other people and, most important for the present study, the knowledge they gain from mass media ultimately providing the context for them to act in accordance with their constructed view of crime. It is important to point out here that although concepts serve a number of important functions in everyday communication and discourse, treating concepts as though they were concrete phenomena leads to the fallacy of reification—the error of regarding abstractions as real rather than as the outcome of thinking.[35] For example, it is erroneous to regard a concept such as "power" as having drives, needs, or instincts, despite the tendency of some people to speak, or write, as if it did. Hence, there is a cyclical effect in constructing the concept of crime in that once people perceive concepts to be real, they go out and look for examples of these concepts.

In the first step of conceptual entrapment by media imagery, many of our observations about crime have something in common. For my purposes, the similarities include the dissemination of images of street crime involving a disproportionate number of African American males. These observations are disseminated through newspaper articles; television reporting; articles on the Internet; speeches made by public speakers, especially political officials; films; radio; books; and music. The crimes depicted include mostly robberies, burglaries, and homicides. Furthermore, as discussed earlier, law enforcement is concentrated in lower-income and minority areas. People who are better off are further removed from police scrutiny and better able to hide their crimes. Although white-collar and elite crime costs society more than street crime, it often goes undetected and is rarely disseminated in mass media. Even when news about white-collar crimes is presented, white-collar offenders are rarely prosecuted and, if they are, they usually receive light sentences—often a fine or community service instead of imprisonment. Thus, the image depicted in mass media of middle- and upper-middle-income people may be perceived as less in need of imprisonment because they likely have a job and high-status people to testify for their good character. On the other hand, when minorities and poor people are accused of a crime, they are more likely to be prosecuted, convicted, and sentenced to prison. Minorities constitute twenty-five percent of the population of the United States but number more than one in three of those people arrested for property crimes and almost one-half of those arrested for violent crimes. African Americans are more than twice as likely to be arrested for crime as are whites.[36] Hence, we begin to find it more convenient to communicate about the general concept of "crime" based on the aforementioned constructions, rather than about the simple content of any single depiction we observe.

The second step of conceptual entrapment by media imagery involves creating a name for the phenomena we have generalized from our specific observations. Because it is inconvenient to keep describing all the specific media depictions, whenever we want to communicate about the general concept they seem to have in common, we give a name to the general concept, in this case "crime," to stand for whatever the specific observations have in common.

In the third step of conceptual entrapment by media imagery, we communicate about the general concept, "crime," and we begin to believe that the concept is something that really exists, not just a summary of several depictions in the media. Thus, when the media refers to "crime" or current "crime reports," we think of the definition we formulated in step 2 and, thus, "crime" becomes real (it matters not that our definition is limited to the general summaries presented by the media in Step 1).

The fourth step of conceptual entrapment by media imagery, now that our concept has become real in our minds, is that we go out in the real world to seek indicators of our term. We write about them, debate them, discuss them; ironically, our indicators are based on depictions we have observed in mass media.

It is important to point out that by presenting the above schema, I am in no way attempting to downplay the importance of concepts in our daily lives; to the contrary, concepts serve important functions not just in everyday life, but in social science as well. Concepts are the foundation of communication:

thinking involves the use of language. Language itself is a system of communication composed of symbols and a set of rules permitting various combinations of these symbols. One of the most significant symbols in a language is the "concept." A concept is an abstraction, a symbol, a representation of an object or one of its properties, or of a behavioral phenomenon. However, it is important to realize that concepts are abstracted from perceptions and are used to convey and transmit information. Concepts do not actually exist as empirical phenomena—they are symbols of phenomena, not the phenomena themselves. In short then, an important merit of the conceptual entrapment by media imagery schema is that it helps elucidate the connectedness of crime and its control with the society from which it is conceptually and institutionally constructed by human agents. Through it, media and crime scholars are able to recognize, as a fundamental assumption, that crime is both in and of society. My wish is that this schema is a first step in abandoning the futile research for causes of crime because such research simply complicates the distinctions that maintain crime as a separate reality while failing to address how it is that crime is constructed as a part of society. Enlightened criminologists are concerned, instead, with the ways in which human agents actively coproduce that which they take to be crime. For instance, this perspective directs attention to the way that crime is constituted as an expansive and permeating mode of discourse, a continuously growing script—a text, narrative—whose writers are human agents, obsessed with what we produce, amazed that it is produced, denying that it is created by us, claiming that it grows independently before us, but yet worshipping the very alienating, hierarchical creations that are our own. A direct consequence of such an approach is that any "frontward analysis" from crime requires that criminologists, law enforcement, media personnel and executives, and criminal practitioners alike deconstruct crime as a separate entity, cease recording it, stop dramatizing it, withdraw energy from it, and deny it status as an independent entity. Through this vision, the present schema may be useful when criminologists begin to record a new ideology, a replacement discourse that connects human agents and our product back to the whole of which we are a part. The conceptual entrapment by media imagery schema, then, is a step in the deconstruction of crime.

NOTES

1. Mark S. Hamm. "The Laundering of White Crime," in Coramae Richey Mann and Marjorie S. Zatz (Eds.), *Images of Color: Images of Crime*, 2nd ed. (Los Angeles, CA: Roxbury, 2002), 218–219.

2. Joseph Melusky. *The American Political System: An Owner's Manual* (New York: McGraw-Hill, 2000), 256.

3. Dennis W. Banas and Robert C. Trojanowicz. *Uniform Crime Reporting and Community Policing: An Historical Perspective* (East Lansing, MI: National Neighborhood Foot Patrol Center, School of Criminal Justice, Michigan State University, 1985).

4. Joseph Sheley. *America's "Crime Problem"* (Belmont, CA: Wadsworth, 1985).

5. See, especially, Douglas A. Smith, Christy A. Visher, and Laura A. Davidson. "Equity and Discretionary Justice: The Influence of Race on Police Arrest Decisions." *Journal of Criminal Law and Criminology* 75 (1985): 234–249; Ronald Flowers. *Minorities and Criminality* (New York: Greenwood Press, 1988).

6. Fox Butterfield, "Racial Disparities Seen As Pervasive in Juvenile Justice," *New York Times*, 26 April 2000, p. 1.

7. Dennis M. Rome. "Murderers, Rapists, and Drug Addicts," in Coramae Richey Mann and Marjorie S. Zatz (Eds.), *Images of Color: Images of Crime*. 2nd ed. (Los Angeles, CA: Roxbury, 2002), 71.

8. The term *lynching* has always been somewhat ambiguous. In the late eighteenth century, it referred to nonlethal summary punishment such as flogging or tarring and feathering. One hundred years later, it meant the summary execution by a mob of an individual who had committed an alleged crime or a perceived transgression of social codes. In 1922, it was defined (in one version of proposed federal antilynching legislation) as "five or more persons acting in concert for the purpose of depriving any person of his life without authority of law" (in a final version, the number of conspirators was changed to three). Twelve years later, a bill before Congress described a lynching as a "mob or riotous assemblage composed of three or more persons acting in concert, without authority of law, to kill or injure any person in the custody of any peace officer, with the purpose or consequence of depriving such person of due process of law or the equal protection of the laws." A federal criminal statute dating from Reconstruction that came to be used against lynch mobs in the mid-twentieth century cited two as the number required to constitute a conspiracy. Today, when lynchings are virtually nonexistent, the term is used primarily as a metaphor, the most well-known example being that of Supreme Court Justice Clarence Thomas who, in his televised confirmation hearing before the Senate Judiciary Committee in 1991, complained that he was the victim of "a high-tech lynching."

The lynching of black Americans was chiefly a Southern phenomenon, but it was not spread evenly across the South. From Tidewater Virginia to Alabama's piney woods, from New Orleans' French Quarter to the Texas ranchlands, the South has always held considerable topographical, social, and political diversity, and lynching statistics reflect it. The Deep South accounts for most lynchings, with Georgia, Mississippi, and Texas the dominant lynching states, followed closely by Louisiana, Alabama, and Arkansas. A majority of lynchings in Tennessee and Kentucky took place along those states' western borders, and in Mississippi, in the densely black-populated area of the Delta. East Texas, more closely aligned in spirit with the Confederate South, saw more lynchings than the western reaches of the state. In general, lynchings were more prevalent in low-lying agricultural lands than in the hills; indeed, they were rare among mountain folk in Kentucky and West Virginia. Despite this diversity, the South often tended to speak with one voice when it came to defending the practice or when threatened by federal antilynching laws.

Philip Dray. *At the Hands of Persons Unknown: The Lynching of Black America* (New York: Random House, 2002), viii and ix.

9. Philip Dray, *At the Hands of Persons Unknown*, ix.

10. *Richmond Planet*, July 11, 1899.

11. Ibid.

12. Ida B. Wells, "How Enfranchisement Stops Lynching," *Original Rights Magazine* (June 1910).

13. W. E. B. Du Bois. *W. E. B. Du Bois Interview: 1960 Oral History Project* (New York: Columbia University Project, 1960), 148.

14. Wells, "How Enfranchisement Stops Lynching," 1910.

15. Ibid.

16. Ibid.

17. Ibid.

18. Ibid.

19. Ida B. Wells. *Southern Horrors & Lynch Law in All Its Phases* (1892). Reprinted in Jacqueline Jones Royster, ed., *Southern Horrors and Other Writings: The Anti-Lynching Campaign of Ida B. Wells, 1892–1900* (Boston: Bedford Books, 1990), 49–52. Wells wrote that 728 blacks had been lynched in the South between 1884 and 1891, with 150 more just in 1892. Only one-third, she said, were charged with rape. Wells herself later increased these figures, saying 1,119 had been lynched between 1884 and 1891, and 160 in 1892. In the year 1890 she would estimate, based on *Chicago Tribune* statistics, that 2,533 Negroes had been lynched in American between 1882 and 1899.

20. The system of race relations that ultimately replaced slavery in the South was the Jim Crow system. Under this system, the minority group is physically and socially separated from the dominant group and consigned to an inferior position in virtually every area of social life. This system was once sanctioned and reinforced by the legal code; the inferior status of African Americans was actually mandated or required by state and local laws. For example, Southern cities during this era had laws requiring blacks to ride at the back of the bus. If an African American refused to comply with this seating arrangement, he or she could be arrested.

21. See, especially, A. Leon Higginbotham Jr. *Shades of Freedom: Racial Politics and Presumptions of the American Legal Process* (New York: Oxford University Press, 1996); Jesse Jackson, *Legal Lynchings: Racism, Injustice and the Death Penalty* (New York: Marlowe and Company, 1996).

22. Katheryn K. Russell. *The Color of Crime: Racial Hoaxes, White Fear, Black Protectionism, Police Harassment, and Other Macroaggressions* (New York: New York

University Press, 1998), 70.

23. Russell, *The Color of Crime*, 70.

24. Kim Curtis, "Prosecutor Shows Oakland Cops' Pattern of Setting Up Suspects," *The Associated Press State and Local Wire* (12 September 2002).

25. Editorial, *New York Times*, 21 November 2002, p. 36.

26. Richard Quinney. *The Social Reality of Crime* (New York: Little Brown, 1970), 15.

27. Quinney, *Social Reality of Crime*, 20–24.

28. Peter Berger and Thomas Luckmann. *The Social Construction of Reality: A Treatise in the Sociology of Knowledge* (Garden City, NY: Doubleday, 1966).

29. Quinney, *Social Reality of Crime*, 22.

30. See, especially, J. Dominick. "A Geographic Bias in National TV News," *Journal of Communication* 27, (1977): 94–99; Doris Graber. *Crime News and the Public* (New York: Praeger Press, 1980).

31. See, especially, Richard Quinney. *The Problem of Crime: A Critical Introduction to Criminology*, 2nd ed. (New York: Harper and Row, 1977); Carolyn Stroman and Richard Seltzer. "Media Use and Perceptions of Crime." *Journalism Quarterly*. 62 (1985): 340–345.

32. Quinney, *Social Reality of Crime*, 262.

33. Patricia J. Williams. "Diary of a Mad Law Professor: Theories of Relativity," *The Nation* (18 November 2002), 9.

34. Russell, *The Color of Crime*, 1998.

35. See, especially, Chava Frankfort-Nachmias and David Nachmias. *Research Methods in the Social Sciences*. 5th ed. (New York: St. Martin's Press, 1996); Earl Babbie. *The Practice of Social Research*. 7th ed. (Belmont, CA: Wadsworth Publishing Company, 1995).

36. United States Bureau of Justice Statistics. (Washington, DC: Department of Justice, 1998).

Bad Boys: Cop-U-Dramas and Other Crime Reality-Based Television Programs

"Reality" police television programs, which showcase black criminals front and center, are another throwback. For instance, on the shows COPS, Final Justice, *and* Highway Patrol, *black suspects are commonly videotaped cursing at law-enforcement officials and otherwise disrespecting the law. The poor, homeless, drug-addicted, mentally unstable, and hardened criminals are lumped together as black crime threats. Shows such as these make it hard to believe that black criminals represent a tiny fraction of the overall black population.[1]*

In October 1989, Charles Stuart, a white, affluent Boston fur salesman claimed that he had been shot and his wife and unborn child had been murdered by an African American male assailant in Mission Hill, a predominantly African American neighborhood.[2] The media portrayed the couple as "starry-eyed lovers out of Camelot cut down by an urban savage."[3] On the other hand, the Mission Hill area was portrayed to the public as "a community run wild with animalistic people."[4]

Mission Hill became occupied territory as Mayor Ray Flynn assigned more police there than had ever been assigned to any Boston community. Hundreds of young African American men were stopped and searched indiscriminately. Public officials called for the reinstatement of the death penalty. Within weeks after the crime, an African American male was apprehended and identified by Charles Stuart as the murderer. The press brushed aside any notion of the suspect's innocence by referring to him repeatedly as the killer.[5]

Several months later, Charles Stuart's brother came forward and revealed that Charles had killed both his wife and unborn child in an effort to profit financially and possibly seek the companionship of another woman. With this admission, the case was solved for many. However, for the residents of Mission Hill and many other African American communities throughout the United States, justice might never be served.[6]

The racist stereotyping of African American citizens has been used as a device by the white power structure to reinforce the subordinate status of minorities throughout American history. Charles Stuart's claim that an African American man had murdered his wife in a poor, African American neighborhood was supported by traditional stereotypes perpetuated by the media and other white-dominated institutions. Thus, Stuart's claim that his family had been murdered—despite his guilt—was transcended by the fact that a poor, African American man was the suspected murderer.

As discussed in chapter 2, negative imaging and stereotyping date back to slavery. Together they served as tools in justifying the total subjugation of Africans by slave traders within the slave system. African slaves were depicted as less than human, non-Christian, and uncivilized. The white slave masters used propaganda to leave the impression that slaves were content with their status in society and could not survive without their masters.[7] Slavery was portrayed as beneficial to male and female slaves so that the white slave masters could protect their cheap source of labor. Whenever the institution of slavery was threatened, the amount and strength of propaganda increased.[8]

After the Civil War, African American citizens held a relative economic advantage over the other ethnic groups; they were experienced farmers in the southern agricultural economy, they constituted most of the skilled workers in the urban South, and they lived close to a growing number of industrial jobs in the North. Fearing competition, however, urban white ethnic groups united in their opposition to hiring African American workers. Racist stereotypes of African Americans served their purpose. As a result of the post–Civil War economy, by 1900, "the class of [African American] artisans had been decimated, reduced from five out of six to only 5 percent in the urban South."[9] In essence, negative imaging and stereotyping were used to maintain the subordinate status of African Americans through low-wage employment.

Today, racist stereotyping of African Americans and other groups has even greater implications, as evidenced by the Stuart case. Jerome Miller, executive director of the National Center for Institutions and Alternatives, believes that the Crime Bill passed during the Clinton administration was driven by the issue of race. Miller contends that since the mid-1980s, for the first time in the nation's history, over fifty percent of the total inmate population was African American.[10] Therefore, he argues, when politicians and the public talk about building more prisons, issuing longer sentences, and putting more police on the street, we are implicitly talking about putting away more African Americans.[11]

As discussed in the previous chapter, the media have the greatest influence on public attitudes about crime; control of information to the public represents control of the public, because people structure many of their views of the world around media information and crime dramatization. The aforementioned conceptual entrapment by media schema suggests that the media tend to influence public perceptions of crime in at least three important ways: (1) by making crime a national problem, (2) by selectively reporting crime news to the public, and (3) by perpetuating criminal stereotypes in the entertainment media.

The evening news is a major instrument of socialization in American society. As such, it helps to determine how an individual sees the world.[12] The prevailing definitions of social reality and social problems, as well as the characterization of groups of individuals, are learned through the process of socialization, and socialization is one of the consequences of media exposure.

The evening news is generally seen as functioning as an agent of socialization in two ways. On one hand, dominant values and attitudes are reinforced during the evening news broadcast when similar values and attitudes are expressed in various formats, explicitly as well as implicitly—explicitly by portraying a disproportionate number of African American offenders on segments such as "Street Sweep," implicitly by using pictures of anonymous African Americans to go with crime commentaries. On the other hand, the evening news might function as a source of norms and values, in that it may provide the initial definitions of social phenomena. For example, where local cultures offer no solid guide for what is good or bad in a particular situation, the media may reach a person directly and exert heavy influence in such value definition.

The segregation and social isolation of African Americans by whites, combined with the inability of social institutions to inform whites about the true sociocultural experience of African American men and women in this country, leave whites to gain much of what they "know" about African American citizens from Eurocentric literature, movies, and television. The media often depict African Americans as being poor, engaged in criminal activity, or on welfare. As a result, ethnicity is confused with stereotypes associated with economic status so that different forms of residential segregation are perpetuated.[13]

REALITY-BASED TELEVISION PROGRAMS

Beginning in the late 1980s, a new trend appeared on television that has continued to the present: reality-based programs. There is a variety of these programs. Some, such as *Jerry Springer*, feature angry confrontations between former lovers or children who claim to be Satanists. *Unsolved Mysteries* features segments on unidentified flying objects (UFOs), the outlaws Bonnie and Clyde, and other popular criminals and crime. Others, programs such as *America's Most Wanted* and *COPS*, are only about crime. In the following section, I will discuss reality-based television crime programs, more specifically, how the image of the African American male as criminal is perpetuated in such programs.

Television programming can be divided into various genres or categories. For example, TV programs could be categorized as situation comedies, police shows, science fiction series, news, talk shows, or game shows. A simpler way of categorizing programs is to make a distinction between fact and fiction. Programs such as *Friends* or *Frasier* are fictional, whereas *The CBS Evening News* and news magazines such as *60 Minutes* claim to present information about real people and events. Other programs are somewhere between TV fiction and the reality of the news. Game shows and late-night talk shows (e.g., Letterman and Leno) are not fiction, but neither are they the news; they are entertainment programming.

Television reality programs are especially hard to categorize because they blur the line between fact and fiction. Programs such as *20/20* cover real people; often, these are celebrities, although occasionally, as in the coverage of the O. J. Simpson trial, stories are about celebrities and crime. Programs such as *Rescue 911* and *America's Most Wanted* reenact actual events.

Perhaps the defining feature of reality television is that these programs claim to present reality. The reality-TV crime programs that are the subject of this chapter claim to present true stories about crime, criminals, and victims. In this, they are a hybrid form of programming: they resemble aspects of the news but, like entertainment programs, they often air in prime time; many are shown as reruns. Moreover, although some of these programs mimic certain forms of crime fiction intended to make them more exciting and to increase their ratings, often the result is presenting a negative image of African Americans.

Two primary formats are used by reality-TV crime programs. Each format bolsters reality claims in different ways. Programs such as *America's Most Wanted* present a series of vignettes in which actors reenact actual crimes. The vignettes feature interviews with victims, their family and friends, the police, and film and photographs of suspects. Viewers are urged to telephone the police or the program with information about crimes or suspects. The programs update previous broadcasts, for example, with film of a captured fugitive or a follow-up if a fugitive is still at large.

Programs such as *COPS* use a second type of format. The TV camera rides with the police and films a story as it unfolds. There is actual footage of the police in action—breaking down a door in a drug bust, or chasing and wrestling a suspect to the ground. The audience sees and hears what the police see and hear. Although this approach is touted as "the real thing," the programs are edited to air the most action-packed sequences. Typically, hundreds of hours of footage are edited each week to produce a single half-hour episode. Editors delete uninteresting video and add clips from a program's file of stock footage.[14]

Two obvious questions are generated by the recent proliferation of reality-based-television crime programs: Why have these programs emerged at this time? Where did they come from? In terms of the "why now?" question, a standard assumption for social scientists is that the social context in which we live informs and shapes everything from what we think about to the nature of our institutions and the policies that drive them. Reality-television crime programs have flourished, in part, because of the social context. Crime policy, ideological notions about crime, and television crime shows are interrelated; they occur within a particular social context.

Newspaper headlines, politicians, and public-opinion surveys reflect a common view about crime today: crime is a serious problem that is getting worse. People are angry and afraid; something has to be done. This view of crime is supported by ideological dimensions that define what we perceive to be the crime problem and the solutions that we consider. To better understand the connections between our view of crime and television depictions of crime, U.S. crime policy since the 1960s must be considered as well as the links between these policies, the social context in which they arose, and media presentations about crime.

The decade of the 1960s was marked by civil disobedience and opposition to authority. The civil rights and women's movements demanded equal rights, and protested laws and policies that blocked those rights. Widespread civil disobedience was common in the opposition to the Vietnam War. In terms of criminal law, the U.S. Supreme Court condemned aspects of the criminal-justice system such as brutal police interrogation techniques and the prison system's almost total control over inmates' lives. To correct abuses within the criminal-justice system, the court emphasized the legal rights of the accused and of prisoners. Rehabilitation was a central tenet of U.S. crime policy. The rehabilitative ideal entailed the belief that factors beyond the individual's control cause criminality. Criminologists said that we could identify the factors, treat them, and cure the criminal of criminality like a doctor cures a patient of a disease. Treatment—on probation, in prison, or on parole—was the order of the day.

Things changed in the 1970s. Politicians and citizens grew concerned about crime. Richard Nixon, who had campaigned on a law-and-order platform, was elected president in 1968 and again in 1972. The U.S. Department of Justice increased federal funding for state criminal-justice systems and extended what had started as President Lyndon Johnson's "war on crime" into the mid-1970s. Criminology also changed its emphasis. Some criminologists criticized the search for the causes of crime: they said that society could not remedy deep-seated social causes of crime. Scholars and politicians advocated policies that vented retributive feelings and that promised to make punishment a more effective deterrent.[15] Although some scholars advocated reduced prison sentences, state legislatures increased them in a get-tough approach in the 1970s.[16]

Ideologically, the 1980s were a repeat of the 1970s. U.S. President Ronald Reagan and British Prime Minister Margaret Thatcher epitomized the continuing shift to the political right. In the United States, people feared that their country, their communities, their values, and their safety were slipping away. Those anxieties helped to produce the "war on drugs," the missing-children issue, the Satanism scare, and an increasing fear of crime.[17] Some of these anxieties and concerns have continued into the new millennium.

The prevailing crime policies and ideologies about crime have changed, but what about the media and how it presents crime? Media critic Steven Stark elaborates on the links among the social context, ideology, and media depictions of crime. Stark notes that during the 1960s, movies with antiauthority themes were common, and lawyer programs were popular on television; however, in the 1970s, TV lawyers were replaced by TV cops, and a concern with civil rights gave way to plots wherein the police violated the law to deliver justice. Stark concludes that, as the public in the 1980s endorsed a crime-control model of law enforcement, television crime shows came to be more about order than about law.[18]

Other scholars agree. Michael Ryan and Douglas Kellner analyze movies in terms of political ideologies. They argue that movies such as *Dirty Harry* (1971) and its sequels attacked a 1960s liberal view of criminal justice that "prevents good cops from doing their job, and . . . lets criminals go free to commit more crimes."[19] *Dirty Harry* and its progeny were conservative law-and-order thrillers that meshed with the times; they were also box-office successes. Even comedy crime movies such as *Beverly Hills Cop* (1984) suggested that bureaucratic rules hamstring the police.

Reality-television crime programs are informed by the conservative ideologies that support current crime policies. Crime is seen as a serious problem, and longer prison sentences, not probation and parole, are offered as the solution. These programs reaffirm Todd Gitlin's notion that, for now, we have abandoned any hope of improving the human condition.[20] Instead, the state is simply trying to maintain order.

So where did reality crime programs come from? There is no single, agreed-upon history behind the recent proliferation of these television shows. In large part, this is because different scholars focus on different aspects of the background of these programs. However, most histories of the media note that television copied much of its programming style from radio.[21] Crime drama was popular on radio; it was dramatic, inexpensive programming.[22] Stark points out that, at first, many radio crime shows were based on novels, short stories, and even comic books that featured private-eye heroes. However, a new type of radio crime program appeared in the 1930s. Beginning with *True Detective Mysteries*, which described an actual wanted criminal at the end of each program, shows such as *Homicide Squad*, *Calling All Cars*, and *Treasury Agent* dramatized real police cases as radio crime entertainment.[23]

Movies are the second link in the chain. Crime films were popular in the 1940s. Although we most often remember Humphrey Bogart movies like *The Maltese Falcon* (1941) or *The Big Sleep* (1946), which were based on private-eye novels, a series of films called "police procedurals" appeared from the mid-1940s into the 1950s. These semidocumentary thrillers drew on FBI and police files or newspaper accounts of actual crimes. Movies such as *The House on 92nd Street* (1945: FBI uncovers a Nazi spy ring), *The Naked City* (1948: tabloid-like film about a murder in New York), and *Dragnet* (1954: Los Angeles Police Department solves a brutal murder) used a narrative style that copied newsreels and World War II documentaries.[24] Filmmakers achieved their documentary look—a gritty realism—by abandoning the Hollywood soundstage in favor of location shooting. The films compromised between a documentary-like emphasis on law-enforcement agencies and the more standard detective-centered drama.[25]

Although the movie *Dragnet* appeared in 1954, the television series *Dragnet* aired in 1951 and ushered in an era of TV crime shows. Like the police-procedural movies, *Dragnet* relied on actual cases and used location shooting and police jargon to create a sense of realism.[26] Its success generated a series of TV clones in the 1950s, including *Highway Patrol*, *Treasury Men in*

Action, and *Night Watch*, which used actual tapes recorded by a police reporter who rode with the police. Another 1950s crime show, *The Untouchables*, evoked a kind of realism because it was about Eliot Ness, a real G-man (government man); it was narrated by newspaper columnist Walter Winchell.[27] Robert Stack, who starred as Ness, would later host *Unsolved Mysteries*, a reality-television crime program.

In the 1960s and 1970s, programs such as *Adam-12* and *Police Story* continued TV's emphasis on law enforcement, and a claim of realism that came from episodes that were based on actual cases. One such program, *The FBI*, profiled wanted criminals at the end of each show. *Hill Street Blues* (1981) perfected the gritty look that movie and television police procedurals had begun years earlier. According to Gitlin, the goal of the producers was to make a show with a realistic texture of sound and visuals. Unusual angles shot with handheld cameras gave it a nervous look of controlled chaos. Actors said their lines as they moved toward or away from the microphone, and unintentionally overlapped their dialogue. An improvisational comedy troupe was hired to generate realistic background hum. *Hill Street Blues* was influenced by *The Police Tapes*, a 1976 documentary film that focused on the police in New York City.[28]

In the mid-1970s, a rather different antecedent to reality crime programs appeared. The *Crime Stoppers* series entailed a brief dramatization of an actual crime followed by a request to help the police solve it. Journalists and police worked together to produce the "Crime of the Week," which was usually aired as a part of a local news broadcast. Crime Stoppers International started the series in Albuquerque, New Mexico in 1976. By 1988, there were 700 programs in U.S. cities, and 29 Canadian programs; they also appeared in England, Sweden, Australia, and Guam. They are still aired today.[29]

United States reality crime television started in 1987 when *Unsolved Mysteries* appeared as a pilot episode. Raymond Burr, who was famous for two TV crime shows, *Perry Mason* and *Ironside*, hosted the pilot. Karl Malden, known for *The Streets of San Francisco*, hosted several follow-up specials. *Unsolved Mysteries* became a regular show in the 1988–1989 television seasons, with Robert Stack as host.[30] *America's Most Wanted* aired on the new Fox network in January 1988. Its creator was familiar with the British and European predecessors, and wanted to Americanize them. The look of *America's Most Wanted* was a combination of 1940s films, MTV music videos, and a gritty realism. *America's Most Wanted* was very successful; it was the first Fox program to beat any of its network competition.[31] *America's Most Wanted* and *Unsolved Mysteries* quickly generated clones, including *COPS*, *Crime Watch*

Tonight, True Stories of the Highway Patrol, American Detective, Untold Stories of the FBI and *Rescue 911*.

CONTEMPORARY EFFECTS

Home security systems, handguns, self-defense courses, and even lifelike male mannequins that ride along in the passenger seat—these are but a few of the hundreds of safety measures that are now common in our crime-apprehensive culture. Despite continued declines in the national crime rate, fear of crime and support for harsher criminal penalties are widespread.[32] According to national polls, more than half of Americans (fifty-five percent) believe that crime has increased in their area of residence, over one-third (thirty-seven percent) name crime as the most important problem facing the country, and the overwhelming majority of individuals (eighty-five percent) believe that the courts are too lenient with criminals.[33] Furthermore, and most important for the present discourse, the sources of fear do not appear to be uniform across demographic categories. Rather, many studies report that fear of crime, especially among whites, is particularly directed toward African Americans.[34]

The obvious question that arises from these national figures, particularly given declining crime rates, is: What explains the public's attitudes and beliefs about crime? Although some attitudes may reflect unfortunate, firsthand experiences with crime victimization, most individuals report that the media serve as their primary source of crime information.[35] What sorts of media provide viewers with information about crime? In the recent past, it is likely that television coverage of actual crime took the form of local and national newscasts. Today, however, "real-life" crime permeates the television environment in the form of entertainment. As one media critic described,

Conspiracies, unsolved mysteries, horrible accidents, missing children, America's most-wanted criminals, and now, real-life beatings, shootings, and violent deaths. When it comes to prime-time entertainment today, these are a few of our favorite things.[36]

Obviously, violence, crime, and mystery have been the focus of many books, films, and television programs predating reality-based programming. However, never before has the viewer been invited along in the squad car or into the scene of a drug bust in the manner encouraged by reality-based programming. In addition, traditional forms of crime-related entertainment do not claim to depict actual crimes in the same way advertised by programs like

COPS, in which the narrator proclaims that the show features "the actual men and women of law enforcement."

Indeed, reality-based police programs are a new and unique genre that blurs the distinction between news and entertainment. Viewers are provided with actual video footage or reenactment of true crimes, and in some instances viewers are encouraged to participate in the capture of criminal suspects by phoning into the program with information that may lead to an arrest. The irony of this new reality-based genre, though, is that it differs considerably from reality in many ways, particularly in terms of the extent to which it overrepresents the frequency of crime. In addition, and germane to the present study, reality-based programs tend to paint a picture of crime in which African Americans, in particular, are cast as evil criminals, or black demons, whereas whites are cast more frequently as the "good guys" or as police officers.[37]

CRIME, RACE, AND TELEVISION

There has long been concern over the representation of minorities in mass media. For much of television's history, as MacDonald notes, broadcasters had been "comfortable with racial stereotyping, whether it was the abrasive representations so abundant in the 1950s or the subtler stylizations of the 1970s."[38] In the early days of television, the series *Amos 'N Andy* portrayed black men as clowns or con men hectored by bossy black women. The problems they confronted in their daily lives were many, although primarily the result of their own ineptitude and unrelated to race.[39] Images of blacks as overly emotional and servile dominated television shows in the 1950s and early 1960s—the few attempts to show blacks in more positive roles were met with resistance by Southern television affiliates, which refused to air them. Because the networks needed to have exposure in as many cities as possible, stereotypical images of minorities acceptable to white Southern audiences dominated.[40] In the 1970s, the image of minorities on television changed dramatically. One reason was the rise of black activism as the NAACP and the Congress of Racial Equality (CORE) helped bring about congressional hearings that criticized the television industry for its inattention to minorities both on the screen and in its hiring practices.[41] Another reason was court rulings dictating that local television stations failing to meet the needs of their communities by acting in a discriminatory manner could have their license renewals denied. The result was that Southern affiliates could no longer refuse to carry television shows on the basis of the racial characters they contained.[42] The primary reason for the rise of positive African American characters in television fiction, however, was the discovery that blacks were heavy users of the medium. "The TV networks . . . turned to black viewers to bolster sagging prime time ratings."[43] Beginning with daytime soap operas in the mid-1960s and continuing through urban dramas such as *I Spy*, *Rockford Files*, *Hill Street Blues*, *Miami Vice*, and *L.A. Law*, blacks began appearing as strong and successful characters—doctors, lawyers, detectives—on television. In fact, *The Cosby Show* in 1984 epitomized the positive representation of African Americans.[44] A transformation also began to take place on television news sets throughout the 1970s and 1980s as well. Local news operations in the vast majority of American communities have hired black reporters and anchors, in part to attract black audiences.[45]

Crime is an extremely popular topic in television fiction. About thirty percent of prime-time television entertainment programming is crime shows, with crime being the most common subject matter for television fiction.[46] Previous content analyses of crime shows reveal an overrepresentation of violent crime. Murder and robbery are the most common forms, with murder accounting for about twenty-five percent of all television crime.

Although images of blacks in television fiction have rarely been positive, stereotypes of minorities as criminals have been uncommon. Studies show that white criminals from higher socioeconomic backgrounds are overrepresented.[47] This is partly because of formula demands; that is, to have powerful, heroic crime fighters, it becomes necessary for them to have formidable foes such as organized-crime figures or business cartels. However, the underrepresentation of minorities as criminals is also because of concern about negative stereotyping of minorities and the potential organized protests that might result. Todd Gitlin notes that standard policies deliberately limited the portrayal of nonwhites as criminals in television shows.[48] Programs such as *Hill Street Blues* that featured black and Latino lawbreakers in an attempt to be "realistic" about crime often had to struggle with network executives and even minority actors on the show to do so.

The nonfiction world of television presents a somewhat more complicated picture of the relationship between race and crime. The amount of attention paid to crime on television news parallels that of fiction television. About ten to fifteen percent of national news involves crime, whereas about twenty percent of local news is crime stories.[49] The image of crime on nonfiction television is similar. J. Sheley and C. Ashkins note that murder and robbery composed about eighty percent of reported crimes on New Orleans' television news, although police data showed them to be far less common.[50]

The picture of crime painted by news reports is somewhat unclear, however. According to Dorris Graber, criminals in the news tend to be either violent street criminals or higher-class property offenders.[51] According to Ray

Surette, criminals shown on the news tend to be slightly older than that reflected in official arrest statistics.[52] Although there is some attention given to white-collar crime, researchers argue that there is an underrepresentation of elite crime. Regardless, although the public may be indignant about corporate crime, it may be safe to assume that it is more concerned about street crime, and street crime, as it is seen in nonfiction television, is primarily an activity of young minority males. Sheley and Ashkins found that blacks accounted for over eighty percent of robbery suspects on New Orleans television.[53] Entman's study of television news in Chicago showed that violent crime committed by blacks accounted for about forty-one percent of all local news stories, and that those stories would suggest that blacks are more dangerous than whites:

The accused black criminals were usually illustrated by glowering mug shots or by footage of them being led around in handcuffs, their arms held by uniformed white policemen. None of the accused white criminals during the week studied were shown in mug shots or in physical custody.[54]

Furthermore, white victimization by blacks appeared to have high priority as news stories.[55] In addition, in the past decade, a new form of "nonfiction" television has emerged: tabloid-style shows that blur even further the distinction between fact and fiction, a trend noted by numerous media scholars.[56] These shows have proliferated, in part, because they are inexpensive and yield relatively high returns in viewership. Most analyses of these shows have been mixed and anecdotal. M. Oliver has done one of the few systematic content analyses of the reality-based police shows *America's Most Wanted*, *COPS*, *FBI, The Untold Story*, and *American Detective*. She found that violent crime was overrepresented, as was the proportion of crimes solved. The shows also presented a world in which white characters were more likely to be police officers, and nonwhites were more likely to be criminal suspects. These depictions were only slight exaggerations from those found in official data. However, Oliver concludes that these programs are more likely to portray "a cast of characters in which nonwhites are typically the 'bad guys,' and a plot that most often features the 'restoration of justice,' although often through aggressive behaviors of heroic white police officers."[57]

At the root of these analyses of race and crime on television is a concern for the impact that these images have on viewing audiences: Do they contribute to concern about crime and foster racist attitudes? Studies of the impact of mass media images on audiences are complex, confusing, and contradictory. A good starting place in examining this issue is the work of George Gerbner and his associates.[58] Gerbner examined the relationship between watching large amounts of television and the viewers' perception of the world. His assumption was that much of television content contained repeated themes, which he identified through "cultivation analysis." Gerbner and his associates began an annual content analysis of television shows in 1968 to identify what they called "cultural indicators," messages about wealth, violence, beauty, power, and prejudice that are portrayed symbolically and may subconsciously influence viewers. These cultural indicators were compared to other measures of the social world, such as those found in government statistics. Finally, survey respondents with varying amounts of television exposure were asked questions about their perceptions of the world. Gerbner and his colleagues found that frequent viewers of television were more likely to have a view of the world that matched the images repeatedly presented through the medium than that reflected by official data (the presumed "real world"). Because violent acts pervaded television, these heavy viewers saw the world as a meaner and more dangerous, crime-ridden place than government statistics suggested.

Other studies have criticized and refined Gerbner's arguments, positing that perceptions of crime are more influenced by the context in which crime and violence are presented. Researchers suggest that when individuals attempt to construct reality, they judge the veracity of media sources.[59] Nonfiction accounts presented by what are considered to be reliable sources have more weight than fictional accounts. Some studies report that if a high proportion of crime news focuses on local crime and portrays it in sensational ways or stresses its random, unpredictable nature, it leads to greater fear of crime among readers or viewers.[60] It is surprising that news of distant sensational crime reduces fearfulness and anxiety about local crime.[61] From these studies, the following three conclusions may be drawn. First, nonfictional images have greater impact than fictional ones.[62] Second, the more a message or theme is repeated, the more influential it becomes. Third, the closer the crime is to home, the more it may generate fear among viewers. Shows such as *COPS*, which are presented as factual, would therefore be more likely than overtly fictional television shows to produce fear of crime.

THE "STREET-SWEEP" STUDY

To provide evidence for some of the aforementioned arguments, Indianapolis's WTHR News Channel 13 was chosen based on its development of a crimewatch segment called "Street Sweep" included in its nightly news broadcast.[63] The segment features snapshots of suspects wanted by Indianapolis police in connection with unsolved crimes. The profiles are received by the station from the combined efforts of Indianapolis police and an FBI task force. The suspects are listed in order of "most wanted" by the task force, who provides the basic descriptions of the individuals for the program. According to sources at the television station, the spots seek to raise awareness of crime within the local community and to provide a service by which citizens can feel like they take an active role in the criminal-justice process.

For analysis, the following definitions were formulated and used in relation to the study

Quantitative bias was defined simply as the inaccurate numerical representation of African American suspects as compared to the national average. If more African American suspects were profiled than are represented in the national population breakdown, then quantitative bias would be noted.

Subjective language was defined as any scripting exceeding the simple details of the appearance of the suspect and the alleged offense. For example, language describing the suspects with familiarity, such as "a good man gone bad" or "needs to be taught a lesson" would be judged as subjective language.

A *negative portrayal* was one reliant on strong, subjective language more than on fact and simple narrative, one that developed a circumstantially negative image of the suspect. For example, descriptions of the personal character of the suspect, such as "not worthy of mercy" or "beyond rehabilitation" would be viewed as a negative portrayal.

Qualitative bias was determined by the definition of subjective language and negative portrayal. The portrayal of African American suspects was compared to that of white suspects and examined for tendencies in language and terminology.

From June to August 1994, twenty-four segments were videotaped as they occurred in the program. For coding purposes, the entire program was taped around the segment to determine where the spot was placed in relation to the relevant news events of the day. The scoring sheet identified segments first by their length in seconds and, second, by their placement within the context of the news program. This method was used to identify the priority assigned to the segment and, thus, the news value attached to it by the station. Also for coding purposes, the programs were divided into four segments: prior to first commercial break, after first commercial, after second commercial, and after third commercial. Most programs were structured in this three-commercial format. Certain "Street Sweep" segments were teased—or introduced—before they were shown. In recording the basic setup of the programs, this feature was also noted. In addition, the particular newscaster who presented the segment was also recorded.

The second half of the coding was performed based on the content of the segment. To this end, the demographic descriptions of both victim (if any) and the suspect were recorded. These demographics included age, gender, racial identification, and social-class background. Further, the segment often used nicknames or identifying features to distinguish the individual being sought by area police. These were recorded when available.

The final area of analysis was the language used to describe the suspects in the course of the segments and to offer details pertaining to their background, character, or tendencies toward violence. Whenever such assertions were made with support from official documentation, this was noted. The newscasters sometimes used voice inflection and suggestive language to express an image of the suspect, for example, regarding one suspect, stating mockingly that the suspect thought he was "tough" and somehow above the law. This particularly scornful quality and similar intonations were noted when presented and evaluated in connection with the language used.

The segments began with a graphic image of a target with an unrecognizable figure behind it representing the suspects being targeted. In addition to the photo mug shot of the suspect, which was shown for suspects both captured and sought, the telephone numbers of the FBI and the Crime Stoppers service were provided on the lower portion of the screen. (As mentioned earlier, "Crime Stoppers" is the name of a series developed by a television station in Albuquerque, New Mexico, as a news-tip/crime hotline for viewers to call in information about the suspects featured.) The same newscaster, a white male, presented all but two of the segments (the others were presented by a white female and an African American male, respectively), adding continuity and a recognizable feature to the series.

FINDINGS

Of the twenty-four newscasts recorded in the two-month period, sixteen segments were broadcast. The segments averaged approximately ten seconds in length. Although a majority of the spots highlighted one particular suspect, two groups of segments (shown together) profiled suspects that had been caught "thanks to the viewers" of these programs. The placement of the segment within the context of the newscast varied little. One segment fell before the first commercial break, nine fell after the first commercial break, six fell after the second commercial break. Although the station regularly runs promotional spots throughout its daily programming to advertise the series, the segments themselves were not usually teased earlier in the newscasts; that is, they were not mentioned and highlighted for viewers to stay tuned. The suspects profiled demographically in these segments as follows: ten African Americans, six whites, fifteen males, one female, two under age twenty, six aged 21–30, five aged 31–40 or older, and three suspects' ages were not given.

Eight of the suspects profiled were wanted in connection with crimes that involved a victim. Another seven were wanted in connection with crimes that had no direct victim mentioned, such as drug use, fraud, or burglary. One segment did not mention the actual crime for which the suspect was sought. Of the crimes that mentioned victims, five of the victims were females, three were male. Four of the victims were white females, and the remaining female victims were not identified by race.

The results of this analysis indicate that the degree of qualitative bias is high for African Americans as hypothesized using the conceptual-entrapment-by-media-imagery postulates. Words and phrases such as "specimen of civility," "Arab individuality," "not worthy of his name," and "thinks he's tough" were used to describe the African American suspects. This finding is very troublesome when one takes into account that the suspects are listed in order of most wanted by the task force who provides the basic descriptions of the individuals for the program. Keep in mind that sources at the television station suggest that the most-wanted list is intended to raise awareness of crime within the local community and to provide a service by which citizens can feel like they take an active role in the criminal-justice process. It is unfortunate that this network is not engaged in any operations to apprehend white-collar offenders in the same neighborhood. As a result of this negligence, the perception of crime presented in this community is only of street crime. Hence, when people in the community think of crime, they will think of street crime, and more egregious, the image of suspects that will appear in their minds will be the image of a black demon.

In addition to qualitative bias, there was significant quantitative bias in the numerical representation of minority suspects. Of the sixteen segments analyzed, ten suspects were African American and six were white[64]—further perpetuating the stereotype of the African American male criminal or black demon.[65]

The regular anchor of the newscast presented more "Street Sweep" segments than any other newscaster. This fact, coupled with the dramatic manner in which they were presented, suggests that the network, or at least the regular newscaster, believes that it is doing its part in the war on crime by informing the public of who the bad guys are. For example, during one episode, the newscaster described Jamok Bobbitt, an African American male accused of selling drugs who also resisted arrest, as a man who "thinks he's tough." It was a rare occurrence for another anchor to present the segment with similarly colorful language. This particular news anchor often takes part in special crime-reporting segments. Thus, the definite quantitative bias of the segments, combined with the qualitative bias present in the negative portrayals, had the net effect of a biased presentation. Although the burden of this bias rested heavily with the quantitative portion of the definition, the result is the same: the continued darkening of the face of crime.

The significant quantitative bias in the series might have serious implications. Entman, for example, argued that such a disproportionate representation contributes to animosity between whites and African Americans. When this animosity drives public policy, the effect is to reinforce the subordinate status of minorities.[66] Moreover, Surette suggested that television programmers could influence public policy when they increasingly focus on crime-related news or other crime shows. Given the early placement of the segment within the newscast, the coverage of local crime is made of primary importance in the news judgment of the station. This crucial placement may either reflect that viewers find crime to be important or dictate to the viewing audience that crime is on the forefront of news issues. In both cases, the news values of the viewer are being shaped and reinforced. Crime becomes extremely relevant, particularly in the local community.

To summarize, reality programming entertains by sensationalizing real stories about crime and justice. It presents actual crime and criminal cases in a realistic light, sometimes in reenactments, sometimes as dramatized stories, and sometimes in documentary-style stories.[67] At the more sophisticated end are the network-produced news-magazine programs, which began with *60 Minutes* and have proliferated into more than a dozen weekly versions. Even these shows, however, have an obsession with violent crime and exploitative stories.[68] This emphasis also contains the most violent content in this genre.[69] What makes these programs worrisome is that they present expanded, in-depth stories that convey the impression that an issue is being discussed from multiple sides. They feel as though they are providing a full context in their coverage, without providing the reality of context. They also amplify the exposure to criminal cases and issues beyond the reporting or viewing of the cases or issues in the media. Viewer preference for reality police programs over fictional crime programming has also been linked with more punitive attitudes about crime and more racial prejudice and authoritarianism.[70] Like most popular news, high-profile, sensationalist crimes and criminals are emphasized with a focus on individual, random, stranger-on-stranger acts of violence. Television news magazines also continue the process of the packaging and marketing of crime information, which has a long history, for popular consumption. They continue to portray the popular culture's perception of crimes and criminals within constructions that are nearly always simplistic and individualistic. At the lower end are programs that are electronic versions of the supermarket tabloid newspapers. These include trash talk shows emphasizing confrontation and sexual deviance, and tabloid news shows emphasizing bizarre violent crimes. These programs are significant in denoting the final phase of a long trend toward merging the once-distinct news and entertainment functions of the mass media.

NOTES

1. Katheryn K. Russell. *The Color of Crime: Racial Hoaxes, White Fear, Black Protectionism, Police Harassment, and Other Macroagressions* (New York: New York University Press, 1998).

2. Ralph C. Gnomes and Linda Faye Williams. "Race and Crime: The Role of the Media in Perpetuating Racism and Classism in America," *Urban League Review* 14 (1) 1990: 57–69.

3. Margaret Carlson. "Presumed Innocent," *Time* (22 January 1990), 10–14.

4. Gnomes and Williams, "Race and Crime," 58.

5. Carlson, "Presumed Innocent," 10.

6. Ibid., 12.

7. Alan Wolfe, (Ed.). "The Enduring Dilemma of Race in America," in Alan Wolfe (Ed.) *America at the Century's End* (Berkeley: University of California Press, 1992), 185–208.

8. Wolfe, "The Eduring Eilemma of Race," 186.

9. Ibid., 187.

10. Rick Szykowny, "No Justice, No Peace: An Interview with Jerome Miller," *The Humanist* 54 (1) January/February 1994: 9–19.

11. Szykowny, "No Justice, No Peace," 10.

12. Dennis M. Rome, "Race, Media and Crime: A Content Analysis of the *New York Times*, the *Atlanta Constitution*, and the *Los Angeles Times* 1950–1988." (Ph.D. diss., Washington State University, 1992).

13. Wornie Reed, (Ed.). *Racial Stereotyping: The Role of The Media* (Boston: William Monroe Trotter Institute, University of Massachusetts, 1990).

14. Debra Deagal, "Tales from the Cutting-Room Floor: The Reality of 'Reality-Based' Television," *Harper's Magazine* (November 1993): 50.

15. James Q. Wilson. *Thinking About Crime* (New York: Basic Books, 1975).

16. Gray Cavender, "A Critique of Sanctioning Reform," *Justice Quarterly* 1 (1984): 1–16.

17. Joel Best. *Threatened Children* (Chicago: University of Chicago Press, 1990); James Richardson, Joel Best and David Bromley, (Eds.). *The Satanism Scare* (Hawthorne, NY: Aldine de Gruyter, 1991).

18. Steven Stark, "Perry Mason Meets Sonny Crockett: The History of Lawyers and the Police as Television Heroes," *University of Miami Law Review* 42 (1987): 220–283.

19. Michael Ryan and Douglas Kellner. *Camera Politics: The Politics and Ideology of Contemporary Hollywood Film* (Bloomington: Indiana University Press, 1988).

20. Todd Gitlin. *Inside Prime Time* (New York: Pantheon, 1983).

21. Eric Barnouw. *Tube of Plenty: The Evolution of American Television*, 2nd ed. (New York: Oxford University Press, 1990).

22. Fred McDonald. *One Nation Under Television* (Chicago: Nelson-Hall, 1990).

23. Stark, "Perry Mason Meets Sonny Crockett," 240–241.

24. Frank Krutnik. *In a Lonely Street: Film Noir, Genre, and Masculinity* (London: Routledge, 1991).

25. Krutnik, *In a Lonely Street*, 203.

26. Stark, 245.

27. Ibid., 247.

28. Gitlin, *Inside Prime Time*, 290–295.

29. Kevin Carriere and Richard Ericson, "Crime Stoppers: A Study in the Organization of Community Policing," (Research Report of the Centre of Criminology, University of Toronto, 1989).

30. Jack Breslin. *America's Most Wanted: How Television Catches Crooks*. (New York: Harper and Row, 1990).

31. Breslin, *America's Most Wanted*, 93–94.

32. Richard Lacayo, "Lock `Em Up," *Time* (7 February 1994), 50–54; "Crime Count," *U.S. News & World Report*, (13 May 1996), 13.

33. Mark Warr, "The Polls-Poll Trends: Public Opinion on Crime and Punishment," *Public Opinion Quarterly* 59 (1995): 296–310.

34. Gertrude L. Moeller, "Fear of Criminal Victimization: The Effect of Neighborhood Racial Composition," *Sociological Inquiry* 59 (1989): 208–221; Elijah Anderson. *Streetwise: Race, Class and Change in an Urban Community* (Chicago: University of Chicago Press, 1990); Craig St. John and Tamara Heald-Moore, "Racial Prejudice and Fear of Criminal Victimization by Strangers in Public Settings," *Sociological Inquiry* 66 (1996): 267–284.

35. Cheryl Russell, "True Crime," *American Demographics* 17 (1995): 22–31.

36. David Zurawik, "Reality TV: Hot Programming Trend Is Changing How Viewers See the World," *Roanoke Times and World News* (Virginia), 23 April 1992, p. E1.

37. See, especially, Jerome G. Miller. *Search and Destroy: African-American Males in the Criminal Justice System* (New York: Cambridge University Press, 1996). In this important piece, Miller contends that our increasing national reliance on the criminal-justice system as the preferred means of dealing with a wide range of vexing social, economic, and personal problems has contributed to racial and social instability. The war on drugs, begun in the Reagan administration and still continuing, has created an explosion in the American prison population, with the number of prison inmates now threatening to exceed the number of students attending college. Whether or not by design, this increase has been accounted for by a severely disproportionate number of African American males. Miller demonstrates that an African American male between the ages of eighteen and thirty-five has an inordinate likelihood of encountering the criminal-justice system at some point during those years.

Miller further contends that the drug war's racial bias has exacerbated an already-present prejudice throughout the criminal-justice system. This bias makes it much more likely not only that young black males will encounter that system, but that they will begin to develop, on the basis of minor offenses more easily plea-bargained than contested, records that result in mandatory prison sentences for any subsequent encounters. The entire system, Miller argues, cascades from a greater likelihood of blacks' initial encounter with the justice system to an increased probability of incarceration for longer and longer periods.

In a wide-ranging survey, Miller describes widespread bias among police officers, probation officers, and courts, whereas social scientists, whose data form the basis for much of the public policy toward crime, and social workers, whose responsibility is allegedly to members of the underclass, have uncritically accepted the questionable assumptions of criminal-justice processing. He warns that the sudden rekindling of interest in genetics and crime, along with the creation of a massive crime-control industry, hold even greater danger for racial minorities in their encounters with the justice system.

38. MacDonald, *One Nation Under Television*, 248.

39. Melvin Ely. *The Adventures of Amos 'N Andy* (New York: Free Press, 1991); MacDonald, 147.

40. Kathryn Montgomery. *Target: Prime Time* (New York: Oxford, 1989).

41. Montgomery, *Target: Prime Time*, 22; MacDonald, 147.

42. Montgomery, 23–24.

43. MacDonald, 248.

44. Michael Parenti. *Make-Believe Media: The Politics of Entertainment* (New York: St. Martin's Press, 1992). Parenti points out, however, that although *The Cosby Show* is an advancement in black imagery, it is a sitcom that "still has Black people playing for laughs." The National Commission for Working Women of Wider Opportunities for Women (WOW) criticized TV for presenting an inaccurate view of racial matters in America, noting that the medium painted a misleading view of a racially harmonious world in which injustice resulted from character flaws rather than social structures.

45. R. M. Entman, "Modern Racism and the Images of Blacks in Local Television News," *Critical Studies in Mass Communication* 7 (4) 1990: 332–345.

46. G. L. Gerbner and L. Gross. "The Violent Face of Television and Its Lessons," in E. Palmer and A. Dorr, (Eds.), *Children and the Faces of Television* (New York: Academic Press, 1980), 149–162.

47. W. J. Potter and W. Ware, "An Analysis of the Contexts of Anti-Social Acts on Prime-Time Television," *Communication Research* 14 (1987): 664–686.

48. Gitlin, 286–324.

49. Dennis M. Rome and Steven Chermak. "Race in Crime Stories," in James Hendricks and Bryan Byers (Eds.), *Multi-Cultural Perspectives in Criminal Justice* (Chicago: C. L. Thomas, 1994).

50. J. Sheley and C. Ashkins, "Crime, Crime News, and Crime Views," *Public Opinion Quarterly* 45 (1981): 492–506.

51. Doris Graber, *Crime News and the Public* (New York: Praeger Press, 1980), 57–58.

52. Ray Surette. *Media, Crime and Criminal Justice: Images and Realities* (Pacific Grove, CA: Brooks/Cole, 1992).

53. Sheley and Ashkins, "Crime, Crime News, and Crime Views," 492.

54. Entman, "Modern Racism and the Images of Blacks," 137.

55. Rome, "Race, Media and Crime, 35.

56. David Altheide. *Creating Reality: How TV News Distorts Events* (Beverly Hills, California: Sage, 1976); Neil Postman and Steve Powers. *How to Watch TV News* (New York: Penguin, 1992); Mark Fishman. *Manufacturing the News* (Austin: University of Texas Press, 1980).

57. M. Oliver, "Portrayals of Crime, Race and Aggression in 'Reality-Based' Police Shows: A Content Analysis," *Journal of Broadcasting & Electronic Media* 38 (2) 1994: 179–192.

58. G. Gerbner and L. Gross, "Living with Television: The Violence Profile," *Journal of Communication* 26 (1976): 173–199; G. Gerbner, L. Gross, M. Jackson-Beeck, S. Jeffries-Fox, and N. Signorielli, "Cultural Indicators: Violence Profile No. 9," *Journal of Communication* 29 (1978): 177–196; G. Gerbner, L. Gross, M. Morgan, and N. Signorielli, "The Mainstreaming of America: Violence Profile No. 11," *Journal of Communication* 30 (1980): 10–29.

59. R. Hawkins and S. Pingree, "Some Processes in the Cultivation Effect," *Communication Research* 7 (1981): 193–226; G. O'Keefe. "Public Views on Crime: Television Exposure and Media Credibility," in R. N. Bostrum (Ed.), *Communication Yearbook 8* (Thousand Oaks, CA: Sage, 1984), 514–537.

60. L. Heath, "Impact of Newspaper Crime Reports on Fear of Crime: Multi-Methodological Investigation," *Journal of Personality and Social Psychology* 47 (2002): 263–276; A. Liske and W. Baccaglini, "Feeling Safe by Comparison: Crime in the Newspapers," *Social Problems* 37 (3) 1990: 360–374.

61. Heath, "Impact of Newspaper Crime Reports," 264.

62. It is important to point out that Parenti and some other media scholars would disagree and perhaps argue that fictional media poses a greater influence on values and beliefs because the audience is less aware of the ideological messages embedded in the texts than is the case for nonfictional media presentations.

63. I presented a version of this study at the Association of Black Sociologists, August 1995, Washington, D.C. in a presentation entitled "The Depiction of African American Criminals in Prime-Time Cop-U-Dramas: A Content Analysis." The data-collection process for this study was made possible, in part, by a grant from Eugene Kintgen, Dean and Director of the Undergraduate Research Partnership Program, Indiana University, Bloomington, Indiana, June 1994. The author would like to especially thank former undergraduate students Shervan Sardar and Robyn Holtzman for their work in the Undergraduate Research Partnership Program.

64. United States Bureau of Justice Statistics. (Washington, DC: Department of Justice, 1999).

65. It is important to point out that although African Americans engage in more violent crimes proportionate to their population size than whites do, the Street Sweep series tends to focus on both violent and nonviolent crimes. Of the sixteen reports, eight were violent in nature.

66. Entman, 333; also refer to Miller, *Search and Destroy*, 98.

67. Mark Fishman and Gray Cavender. (Eds.) *Entertaining Crime: Television Reality Programs* (New York: Aldine De Gruyter, 1998).

68. C. Whitney, E. Wardwell, D. LaSorsa, W. Danielson, A. Olivarez, R. Lopez, and M. Klihn, "Television Violence in 'Reality' Programming: University of Texas, Austin Study," in *National Television Violence Study*, vol. 1 (Thousand Oaks, CA: Sage, 1997), 269–304.

69. M. Oliver, "Portrayals of Crime, Race, and Aggression, 179–192.

70. M. Oliver and G. Armstrong. "Predictors of Viewing and Enjoyment of Reality-Based and Fictional Crime Shows," *Journalism Quarterly* 72 (1995): 559–570.

Bamboozled: Criminal Stereotypes of African Americans in Cinema

The success of Sweet Sweetback's Baadasssss Song, Shaft, *and* Superfly *snapped the industry moguls to attention. Soon black films began turning up with startling regularity. Sometimes it even looked as if the same movies were being remade time and again. First there was* The Legend of Nigger Charley *(1972), then* The Soul of Nigger Charley *(1973). There were* Black Caesar *(1973),* Black Sampson *(1974),* Black Jesus *(1971), and* Sweet Jesus, Preacher Man *(1973). There were* Slaughter *and* Slaughter's Big Rip Off *(1973, an appropriate title if there ever was one), also* Blacula *and* Scream, Blacula, Scream *(1973). There were also* The Bus is Coming *(1971),* Top of the Heap *(1972),* The Final Countdown *(1972),* Hit Man *(1972),* Cool Breeze *(1972),* Detroit 9000 *(1973),* The Black Godfather *(1974), and* The Mack *(1973).*

What became most disturbing was that while these movies appeared to be black (in concept, in outlook, in feel) and while they were feverishly promoted and advertised as such, they actually were no such thing. Many of the new black-oriented films were written, directed, and produced by whites. . . . Worse, many of the new movies were often shot on shoestring budgets, were badly directed, and were technically poor. The film industry hoped simply to make money by indeed exploiting an audience need. Eventually, there was the rise of what came to be known as the blaxploitation film: *a movie that played on the needs of black audiences for heroic figures without answering those needs in realistic terms.*[1]

BLAXPLOITATION FILMS AND THEIR PROLIFERATION OF THE BLACK DEMON

At first glance, it appears that with the new millennium came a spurt of progress in the film industry because three African Americans—two men, Denzel Washington and Sidney Poitier, and a woman, Halle Berry—won the industry's highest award: an Oscar. After closer examination, one finds that the negative stereotypes of yesteryear are perpetuated in the films that won Denzel and Halle their awards (Poitier was awarded an Oscar for his long and illustrious career in cinema).[2] Washington won an Oscar for best actor in *Training Day*, in which he played an extremely violent rogue cop who dealt drugs and, although he was married and not estranged from his wife, kept another woman and their child in an apartment in the ghetto. Berry won best supporting actress for her role as an overly sexed temptress in *Monster's Ball*, in which she has wild, passionate sex with the bigoted prison guard who executed her husband. Consistent with the theme of the present study, contemporary cinema, despite its seeming spurts of progressive surface appearance, continues to perpetuate the myth of the black demon; drugs, crime, and an abundance of sex seem to be associated with African Americans in many of Hollywood's contemporary films. Many scholars of film agree that the catalyst for this phenomenon began during the period between 1971 and 1976 now referred to as the blaxploitation era of American cinema.[3]

The turbulent social times of the 1960's especially the signing of the Civil and Voting Rights Acts (1964 and 1965, respectively), the assassinations of Malcolm X (1965), the Reverend Martin Luther King Jr. (1968), and John and Robert Kennedy (1963 and 1968), spun a newfound form of activism. Student protests against the Vietnam War, the establishment of black nationalist parties—especially the founding of the Black Panther Party—and the rising consciousness of women and their demands for equality did not conform or agree with the prevalent images and stories shown in Hollywood cinema. As a result, a plunge in box-office receipts for Hollywood executives forced them to rethink their storylines and images. Some film companies were contemplating closing their doors and it is even reported that one company sold the ruby slippers worn by Judy Garland in *The Wizard of Oz* for $20,000 just to keep their doors open. Hence, while Hollywood executives were spinning their wheels about what new genres might attract moviegoers Melvin Van Peebles, who received modest recognition for his film *Watermelon Man*, in which a white bigot wakes up black and consequently loses his family, house, job, and friends, brought *Sweet Sweetback's Baadasssss Song* to a limited number of theatres. In a similar way, Gordon Parks was summoned to produce and direct *Shaft*, a feature-length film originally made for an all-white cast and changed by Hollywood executives to cash in on the success of *Sweetback*.

These movies of course, reflected the shifting outlooks and attitudes of Americans, especially African Americans. Indeed, no other period in black movie history has been quite as energetic or important as the blaxploitation era. More black actors and actresses worked in films than ever before; African American writers such as Richard Wesley, Bill Gunn, and Lonne Elder III wrote scripts for important productions; and such black directors as Gordon Parks Sr. and Gordon Parks Jr., as well as Sidney Poitier, Michael Schultz, Stan Lathan, Hugh Robertson, and Ossie Davis all made major studio films. Indeed, for the first time in film history, the studios produced black-oriented films pitched directly at pleasing blacks—and all audiences saw black movie characters speaking in a new idiom and rhythm. Movies sought to give some semblance of a black community with a set of attitudes, aspirations, and grievances all its own.[4]

SWEET SWEETBACK'S BAADASSSSS SONG

Although images of the 1970s were far different from those of previous decades, often enough the old stereotypes resurfaced, simply dressed in new garb to look modern, hip, provocative, and politically "relevant." The early years of the era contributed most to the image of the black demon, a period during which a band of aggressive, pistol-packing, sexually charged urban cowboys and pimps set off on a charge, out to topple the system and to right past wrongs. Enters Melvin Van Peebles's 1971 film *Sweet Sweetback's Baadasssss Song*. This film introduced a new version of the black demon that was more defiant and devious than ever. When Van Peebles began making this film, he had four criteria that he wanted his new-wave film to fulfill. During an interview that preceded the film, he talked about what he hoped the film would accomplish and how he felt about the film itself. First and foremost, Van Peebles wanted to create a film that was not a cop-out. This film had to overcome the normal stereotypes of the black race. It could not give in to the old ways of portraying blacks as servants and the like. Van Peebles wanted blacks to be seen in a whole new light. He wanted them to take on a new identity, one that they created for themselves. Second, this film had to "look" as good as anything "the man had ever done." This film had to rate up there with the best of films that white directors had made. This could not be just another black-produced film that was passed over. This film had to grab everyone's attention because of its quality and style. For once, according to Van Peebles, a black filmmaker had to outdo "the man."[5] Third, Van Peebles wanted this film to be noticed and something that the African American people could be proud of. The fourth thing he hoped this film would accomplish was that it would serve as a "living workshop." He wanted individuals to watch this film and learn from it. He hoped that black producers would take this lead, follow in his footsteps, and make other films that African Americans could relate to and feel proud about. Melvin Van Peebles attempted to take the film industry of the day and turn it completely around.[6] Did he succeed? Or did he inadvertently contribute to the criminal stereotypes of African Americans?[7]

Van Peebles's *Sweet Sweetback's Baadasssss Song* was the first film that portrayed an extremely sexual black man as the lead character. The main character of the film, Sweetback, became the black demon of the times dressed in fancy clothes, sleeping with countless women and often receiving money for his services. His story was that of a life on the run, which unfolds after he witnesses two white police officers beating a black youth in their custody. After Sweetback watches the beating for a few moments, he knows that he has to do something to stop the officers. Out of rage, Sweetback takes matters into his own hands and begins beating the officers in the heads with their own handcuffs. After this, Sweetback is no longer allowed to wander the streets freely. Now that he is wanted by officials for killing two officers, he must live his life on the run. He must always live with the fear that the police will one day catch up with him. Sweetback running from the police, stopping occasionally to have sex with many different women, constitutes the remainder of the film. This sequence of events continues on throughout the film, which concludes with the message "A Baadasssss Nigger is Coming Back to Collect Some Dues" as Sweetback is still seen running from the police.[8]

Despite the fact that Van Peebles followed a popular trend during this time in Hollywood films of depicting the violent and hypersexed African American male, sadly, it surprisingly received great support from black audiences as well as from some young white audiences. What made this particular film so popular was that it showed a powerful black man who was finally able to triumph over the white man. Although Sweetback was a criminal, he was still a hero to many; for the first time on the big screen, the black man had outsmarted the white man. Sweetback had stood up for what he believed and won. The African American community finally had a triumphant figure through Sweetback. However, the way in which the African American male is portrayed in this movie leads the audience to have a pervasive negative image of African American males; worse, such films reinforce the black demon stereotype. This film follows Sweetback as he breaks laws and runs from the police, thus presenting characteristics to be feared rather than respected and admired.

SHAFT

Another popular film produced during the 1970s, which made use of the *black demon* stereotype, was Gordon Parks' *Shaft*.[9] John Shaft, the main character in *Shaft*, was portrayed as a powerful black man that was on the good side of the law. He was assertive and kowtowed to no one, not even to the main white characters in the film. At first look, one might argue that the images portrayed in *Shaft* are positive and a great departure from the images in *Sweetback*. However, after a closer look, one sees Shaft portrayed as an oversexed black demon, constantly sizing up women and frequently making remarks about women as sexual objects. Shaft's sexual attraction to white women fits into the stereotype of the hypersexed black buck—lusting after white women. The only extended contact Shaft had with women was when he was engaging in sex with them. Other than as objects for sexual pleasure, women had no role in the film.

Because of the success of Quentin Tarantino's *Jackie Brown* (1997), a film that supposedly pays homage to blaxploitation films, a remake of *Shaft* by African American producer John Singleton stormed the theatres in 2000.[10] In Singleton's version, Samuel L. Jackson portrays Shaft's nephew, a New York cop who quits the force in disgust to track down a bail-jumping, racist, rich, white kid (played by *American Psycho*'s Christian Bale) charged with killing a black man. In the new *Shaft* film, Shaft also has to locate the one woman who witnessed the murder, a fearing-for-her-life bartender played by Toni Collette. Vanessa Williams plays Shaft's cop buddy, and rap singer Busta Rhymes portrays a streetwise cohort. Singleton is quoted as saying the following about the new Shaft persona: "It's attitude—looking good and being bad. . . . Sam is the only actor who could've pulled it off. He's the coolest actor on the planet."[11] New persona? Unfortunately, Shaft is quoted in the new version as saying, "It's my duty to please the booty."[12] Again, this sounds like more of the hypersexed black demon characteristics true to the blaxploitation period it is emulating.

For the most part, women had very few roles outside of being prostitutes and drug addicts in films during this period. Perhaps the most famous African American female star of this period is Pam Grier, whose body was overexposed and exploited in films such as *Cleopatra Jones* (1973), *Coffy* (1973), *Foxy Brown* (1974), and *Black Mama, White Mama* (1973). In *Coffy*, Grier plays a vigilante, of sorts, who combs the ghetto looking for the drug pushers who sold drugs to her younger sister who died from an overdose. The sex and violence in many of these films is gratuitous to say the least. Aside from X-rated films, there were very few films (if any) during this time that depicted white women in such negative and degrading roles.

SUPERFLY

Among films of the 1970s that portrayed African American males as criminals was *Superfly*.[13] *Superfly's* main character is Priest, a well-known, big-time Harlem drug dealer. Priest spends his days, as well as his nights, selling and organizing the delivery of drugs. He is so prominent in the drug business that he has several individuals working under him who actually do the drug deals for him; Priest is sort of an overseer who is portrayed as ruthless and uncaring about anyone except himself. This movie glamorizes the drug industry by depicting Priest having all of the material possessions he wants. He is shown wearing the best clothes, driving very expensive cars and, of course, always having a beautiful woman by his side. Here again the stereotype of the black demon emerges—Priest is overly promiscuous and has two different female lovers, neither of whom he is faithful to. As in the blaxploitation films to follow, women in *Superfly* are not only marginalized, but they are seen only as sexual beings and only when they are in the presence of men.

Priest is also depicted as a heavy drug user in this film. Whenever Priest is on the screen for any extended period of time, he is shown snorting cocaine. The false sense of success that is being presented here is especially detrimental to African American youth. At one point in the film, Priest confides to his friend Eddie that he wants to get out of the game. Eddie laughs and says he cannot believe that Priest wants to give up the good life: "eight-track stereo, color television in every room and an endless supply of cocaine."[14] According to Eddie, this is the "American dream." When so few positive African American role models exist and our young people are exposed to such images— images that suggest that all blacks should strive for is material possessions and drugs—this misconception of achievement and attainment legitimizes the present unequal status of African Americans today.

Other films produced in the blaxploitation period further perpetuated the criminal stereotype of African Americans: oversexed, criminal and, especially, drug-addicted. So, although this era opened up a different technique of film-making, film producing, and directing, sadly, these films perpetuated the stereotypes depicted as early as the negative stereotypes in *Birth of a Nation* and some film historians argue that the blaxploitation period is among the worst in the film industry's depiction of African Americans as criminals. It is important to point out that although the fashion and music from these films had a major impact on popular culture during this time, and even if people flocked to the theaters to listen to the music or to witness the latest fashion, they were still bombarded with degrading stereotypes of African Americans and, unfortunately, although a handful of other films depicted blacks in more realistic and humanistic roles, the *Sweetback, Superfly* and *Shaft* remakes outnumbered them dreadfully. Many film critics agree that although more blacks graced the silver screen during the blaxploitation period, they were relegated to roles that made them appear more homogeneous, thus giving the impression that all blacks behaved in these ways. Worse, whereas whites already know that the members of their group come in all moral and intellectual shapes and sizes, they know much less about blacks. The blaxploitation films therefore reinforced whites' ignorance of blacks' variety and humanity.

CONTEMPORARY IMAGES

Contemporary images in Hollywood of African Americans are a mixed bag. On one hand, black characters portray old derogatory stereotypes of yesteryear such as Cuba Gooding's character in *Lightning Jack* (1994), in which he portrayed a modern-day "coon" by rolling his eyes and shuffling his feet, and Willard Pugh's role as Detroit mayor in *RoboCop 2* (1990)—a role that some movie-goers in Detroit argued was racist. There was Warren Beatty's political parody *Bulworth* (1998), in which childlike black characters pandered to their great white figure, the politician Bulworth. And *The Green Mile* (1999), in which actor Michael Clarke Duncan plays the role of a prisoner on death row in Louisiana accused of having raped and murdered two nine-year-old white girls. He refers to the prison guards as "Boss" and is later revealed to have healing powers that he used to help his white oppressors. Elvis Mitchell, film critic of the *New York Times* wrote that *The Green Mile* pushed "across the boundary between a movie about racism and a vaguely racist movie."[15] Similar to *The Green Mile* is *The Legend of Bagger Vance* (2000), in which Matt Damon, a one-time golf champion, struggles to get his old game back to enter a championship tournament. Quick to the rescue is Bagger Vance, played by Will Smith, who offers to caddy for Junuh (Matt Damon) for five dollars—less than the standard 10 percent of the tournament purse that most caddies get. Like the main black character in *The Green Mile*, through the use of magical powers, Bagger helps Junuh get his swing back and all is well in Louisiana:

Poor deluded Bagger seemed part noble tom, part adoring nurturing mammy, and most times downright laughable. *Newsweek*'s David Ansen described Vance as "a cross between Krishnamurti and Uncle Ramus." One only wonders why the black Bagger isn't prone to helping any black people solve their problems, especially since this is the apartheid south of the Great Depression era. One cannot help but agree with the *Washington Post*'s Rita Kempley who wrote that "nobody connected with this sap-oozing fantasy seems to have taken the time or the place into consideration. . . . director Robert Redford plays possum when it comes to racism." Kempley also referred to "the degrading aspects of Smith's role," adding, "Isn't it time to put Stepin Fetchit to rest?" Like the character in *The Green Mile*, Vance might not have been meant to be taken as a real person "but a spiritual emanation," wrote the *New York Times*' A.O. Scott. "But supernatural is not much better than subhuman: Hollywood is still, in the year 2000, disinclined to let black actors play human beings."[16]

In *The Patriot* (2000), although the horrors of the American Revolutionary War were depicted, the producers still managed to depict happy slaves on plantations. One film critic is quoting as saying, "[*The Patriot*] is civics-lesson condescension."[17] The black demon stereotype managed to surface in a well-received film like *Traffic* that depicted contemporary drug trade in the United States. When the daughter of the antidrug czar in the film wants drugs, where does she go? To the African American ghetto, of course. There she is greeted by the stereotype of the African American male "buck" and just minutes before he is to rape her she is saved by her father.

Director and producer Quentin Tarantino played a major role in reintroducing the blaxploitation genre to a new and young audience with his film *Jackie Brown* (1997). Pam Grier stars as a flight attendant who is caught smuggling $500,000 into the country. The plot unravels as Grier plays the mob boss, for whom she works, off federal agents. Like earlier blaxploitation films, the Tarantino film is riddled with negative depictions of African Americans—his use of a "soul" soundtrack featuring the Delfonics, the Brothers Johnson, Bobby Womack, and Bill Withers cannot save the damaging images on the screen. As is earlier blaxploitation films, the soundtrack had very little to do with the poorly written story along with its gratuitous scenes of sex and violence. In addition, Tarantino did something that no other white filmmaker ever attempted: he had the main character (Samuel L. Jackson) use the word *nigger* in almost every sentence he spoke. Film critics and filmmakers alike were outraged with Tarantino's obsession with the "N word." One of the most outspoken opponents was filmmaker Spike Lee, who argued that when he used the term *nigger* in his films that he used it as part of his in-group lexicon—it is another matter when an outsider feels he has the right to toss the word about.

After the moderate success of *Jackie Brown*, other studios tried their hands at contemporary blaxploitation ventures. *I Got the Hook-Up (1998)* is another modern blaxploitation film that portrays two African American men as black demons, Black and Blue, as they make their living from being the best con artists in the "hood."[18] Their specialty is selling hot merchandise cheaply at their "shopping center" in the ghetto. People come from all over town to purchase their goods—they can get anything a person wants and at the best price. Their business is excellent until they establish their own line of credit, which they extend to their best customers. Business is booming for Black and Blue and gets even better when they encounter a lost delivery truck and convince the driver that the merchandise aboard is meant for them. The merchandise happens to be cell phones, which Black and Blue begin marketing at an extremely low price; soon nearly everyone in the hood has a cell phone. When the cell phones begin to malfunction, Black and Blue find themselves on the run—the film becomes a typical chase film. This film lacks plot and perpetuates the stereotypes of early blaxploitation films by depicting Black and Blue as jobless, conniving, and on the run from the law. Similarly to earlier films, the role of women in *Hook-Up* is nothing more than as sex objects: they are often portrayed as "bitching," they wear very seductive clothing and, basically, they are time fillers.

Another recent film is *Belly*[19] (1998), a film that continues the negative stereotypes of African American males as criminals—drug-dealing hoodlums, to be exact. Dealing drugs is the only way of life for the main characters in this film. They are portrayed as extremely tough thugs who do not care about anything but making the drug deal. One character, Sincere, is portrayed as caring for his family. In fact, he talks about getting out of the drug business and escaping to Africa were he believes his family could live in a drug-free and crime-free environment. Of course, women are again portrayed as sex symbols having very few lines and usually seen only when they are with men or when they are talking about men.

In another film, *The Long Kiss Goodnight* (1996), Samuel L. Jackson plays Mitch, a private investigator who has been hired to assist a white female victim of focal retrograde amnesia.[20] The character Mitch represents the stereotypes of a scamming, sexually obsessed, stupid thief. During a candid moment between Mitch and the amnesia character, he recounts that his past career as a police officer ended as a result of his four-year incarceration for theft of police evidence (savings bonds). This fact is punctuated when Mitch starts off recounting the incident as if he had been set up by his partner. When his client expresses her condolences about him being set up, he responds, "Aw, naw. I stole the damn things." This dialogue suggests much more than is obvious—it suggests that black criminal behavior is not the result of the system or "the man," as is commonly claimed; rather, it is blacks who are simply looking for someone else to blame and are living in denial about their criminality.[21]

In the film *Sneakers (1992)*, Sidney Poitier plays Donald Crease, a member of a team of renegade hackers routinely hired to test security systems.[22] The construction of Crease is mostly consistent with notions of black criminality in terms of his propensity toward violence and his intellectual inferiority. Crease is the team's security specialist (i.e., the primary gun toter), a fact that associates him with the idea of violence. He is also the only one on the team whose value is not found in technical wizardry. His professional dialogue, consisting largely of things such as directions on how to secure buildings and announcements regarding danger, is made to appear almost elementary when it is juxtaposed against the backdrop of the other members' techno-jargon. This contrast alludes to the idea of Crease's lesser intelligence.

One scene in particular draws attention to this lack of technical knowledge on Crease's part through comedic mockery. On one occasion, Martin (Robert Redford), the leader of the team, has infiltrated a secured facility but is unable to circumvent a coded security lock on an interior door. He communicates this fact by wire back to the team outside in the tech van, and Crease gives him a suggestion. We as viewers are not allowed to hear Crease's recommendation, but it soon becomes evident: after nodding and muttering "okay" several times, Martin concludes with "I'll give it a try" and proceeds to kick the door in.[23]

The discovery of covert stereotyping in this scene requires careful reading, because there are ways in which this scene could be read as devoid of stereotypes. However, the underlying theme, one may argue, is that society has become excessively technical (the kicking-in of the door is an especially low-tech solution). One may also offer that Crease's suggestion, since effective, indicates his superiority in problem solving. Two facts weaken both of these assertions. First, as a low-tech security person, kicking down a door is reasonably read more commensurate with Crease's professional aptitude than representative of his higher analytical skills. Second, kicking down a door is in fact a violent, destructive act, not readily associated with intellectual activity but, rather, with criminal activity (such as burglary).

The film depicts Crease as especially adept at handling violent encounters, super-bad, as it were. In one instance he remarks to the crew, "You guys'll be chalk outlines without me."[24] Later in the film, he single-handedly disarms one shotgun-aiming guard, and then uses it to knock both its owner and his partner to the ground in no time. A bystander's verbal expression of amazement is added to ensure that the magnitude of Crease's super-bad deed is not lost on us.

The film also suggests that Crease has been immoral. Audience interest in knowing why Crease no longer worked for the Central Intelligence Agency (CIA) was set up throughout the entire film. When asked directly, Crease refused to answer. At one point, Martin was even approached by government agents asking about Crease's mysterious dismissal from the agency. At the end of the film, it is revealed that he was dismissed because of his problems associated with an excessive temper (the image of the violent, raging black male). If one is dismissed by the CIA, whose own reputation is shady at best, one's character would have to be seriously questionable. Crease's animalistic rage eventually finds expression on the screen when he beats the aforementioned perpetrators and growls, "You motherfuckers mess with me I'll split your heads!"[25] One may ask how Crease's character can be labeled as negative stereotype when all of the team had been in jail or was running from the law? The answer is that technological-related crime, the only type of crime for which the team members had been in trouble, is not viewed by the majority of society as being comparable to violent crime.

In *Men in Black*[26] (1997), Will Smith plays Jay, a New York police officer who is recruited for extraterrestrial-related government service. Smith's character is stereotyped in two major ways: the film alludes to the ideas of both Jay's supernormal physical ability, implying he is not human, and his propensity toward violence. Jay came to the attention of government recruiter Kay (Tommy Lee Jones) after Jay attempted to arrest a suspect who turned out to be an alien. In a lengthy action scene, Jay chased the alien and pulls off all kinds of daring feats during the pursuit, among which was his leaping from a bridge to a moving trolley with no consequent injury. As he dismounts the trolley, he cracks to the alarmed white passengers, "it just be rainin' black people in New York."[27] Although the writers and producers used this line for humorous effect, the statement can distract one's attention from the question of how Jay manages to avoid injury on the jump. Jay and the fleeing alien are, in a sense, playing "Simon Says": The alien jumped off the bridge first, and Jay followed in pursuit. The back-to-back shots of the two jumps seemed to encourage a comparison between the feat of the alien and the matching feat of Jay. It is this kind of more subtle stereotype that exemplifies the writer's thesis. Undoubtedly, the producers of the film would claim that this sequence of shots was merely intended to illustrate the protagonist's tenacity.

Jay eventually catches the alien who, at one point during the pursuit, scurried up the outside of a skyscraper to the rooftop. When Jay breaks into the building to take the stairs up (another display of tenacity), the shot reveals the upward-spiraling, seemingly never-ending flights of stairs. When this alien, who scaled the outside of the skyscraper at lightning speed, reaches the rooftop, Jay is already there with his gun drawn, not even breathing hard, and remarking, "What's up?"[28]

Later, during an investigation interview (the alien leaped from the rooftop to his death and Jay is being questioned about it), Jay reports that the suspect had blinked two pairs of eyelids. Jay was later informed by Kay that the suspect's eyelids were actually gills, and that "he was out of breath." Out of breath? A skyscraper-scaling alien? It apparently was not enough that the black cop caught a warp-speed alien, but the alien had to be physically exhausted afterward. The producers, I am certain, would again beg to differ, arguing that the physiology of this particular life form is comparable to that of humans, so it was capable of getting winded. The writer supposes that its muscular system just happened not to be comparable. A later statement by Kay eliminates any doubt with regard to the message being communicated: "This kid ran down a cephalopoid on foot. . . . That's gotta be tough enough" (Kay made this statement on two different occasions).[29]

Jay is also depicted as a smart-talking black man with an attitude problem ("he's got a real problem with authority"). An iterated element in the film is his standing nose to nose with adversaries (in one instance, a huge alien) and warning them to "back up outta his face." His tendency toward hostility is most overtly represented by his shooting of a target made up to resemble a young white girl, instead of the vicious monster targets that surround it. In self-defense he states:

[E]ight-year-old white girl, middle of the ghetto, bunch of monsters, this time of night, with quantum physics books. . . . She 'bout to start some shit. . . . Those books are way too advanced for her. . . . If you ask me I think she's up to something, and to be honest I'd appreciate it if you eased up off my back about it.[30]

Although this episode appears to be flattery on one hand (Jay was able to figure out a difficult situation), on the other hand, it is an example of covert negative stereotypes (a hostile black cop with an attitude problem who shoots, and justifies killing, a small white girl).

Media scholars Robert M. Entman and Andrew Rojecki remind us that:

[T]he dominant movie images of blacks still create voids where white viewers might potentially find more consistent challenges and correctives. Different kinds of movies could nurture the more positive side of whites' ambivalent ledgers, their empathy, hope, and yearning for connection. We do not mean to suggest that having big-budget movies with African Americans as "positive role model" and heroes of complexity would by itself significantly alter race relations. Rather, the scarcity of such films records as it contributes to the persistence of misunderstanding, stereotypes, and animosity.

We recognize the complicated task that the film industry faces. Part of the reason for the movie images of blacks lay in the way stereotypical movie representations interact with human perception. In a sense, each member of the ethnic group bears the burden of representing his or her entire category. For some film viewers, if a character conforms in any way to negative stereotypes, that is what they will notice and remember; they will disregard any nonstereotypical qualities the same character demonstrates.[31]

Hence, it is simply not enough to have African American directors and producers. Perhaps there should be a greater focus on independent films, for which funding often is mainly from grants and endowments so that the amount of profit would not drive the content of the film, and the number tickets sold during opening night therefore would not determine the fate of the film. Moreover, perhaps filmmaking should not be approached to appeal to a large audience; instead, shorter, more tailored, films may contribute to debunking some of the negative stereotypes for African Americans. It is important to point out that although black actors and actresses, directors, producers, and other film personnel were hired in unprecedented numbers during the blaxploitation era, these films were still negative in depiction. In a similar way, the New Jack films of the 1980s involved many people of color—but they especially exploited "the hood" and definitely painted the picture of drug users as predominately African Americans. This is especially ironic in light of the social and political gains made during the 1990s for many African Americans; it seems that the negative imagery continues, at least in the film industry. The stereotypes that grew from the blackface performances of long ago are still present in contemporary films. These representations paint a much distorted picture of what the African American way of life is really like. In reality, whites and blacks both have very similar ways of life. As mentioned in earlier chapters, white Americans use more illicit drugs than blacks; yet, there is little to suggest this in contemporary films. Until the structure of the film industry changes, this unfair and distorted pattern will continue to paint African American males as criminals—black demons.

NOTES

1. Donald Bogle. *Toms, Coons, Mulattoes, Mammies, and Bucks: An Interpretive History of Blacks in American Films*, 3rd ed. (New York: Continuum, 2002), 241–242.

2. "Blaxploitation" has also been defined as a commercial-minded film of the seventies for black audiences. See, especially, Isaac Julien's *Baad Asssss Cinema: A Bold Look at 70's Blaxploitation Films*. The Independent Film Channel: Minerva Pictures Production, 2002.

3. Julien, *Baad Asssss Cinema*. Filmmakers and critics such as Elvis Mitchell of the *New York Times*; Afeni Shakur, mother of the late rap artist Tupac Shakur; Quentin Tarantino, filmmaker of *Jackie Brown* fame; Melvin Van Peebles; Pam Grier; and Fred Williamson, as cited in Isaac Julien's documentary have agreed with this perception.

4. Bogle, *Toms, Coons, Mulattoes, Mammies*, 234–235.

5. Ibid, 234–235.

6. Ibid.

7. In a conversation I had with Melvin Van Peebles in spring 2002, during his tenure as a visiting Professor of Film for the Department of Afro-American Studies and the Black Film Archives at Indiana University, Bloomington, Van Peebles stated that the success of *Sweetback* was due largely to the fact that the FBI tried to prevent having the film shown in a wide distribution because members of the Black Panther Party required its viewing for all of its members. As a result, people came out to see what the FBI was trying to censor. Afterward, Van Peebles stated that the film took on a life of its own and the reviews of film critics, both good and bad, added to the film's box-office attraction.

8. *Sweet Sweetback's Baadasssss, Ass Song*, dir. Melvin Van Peebles, 97 min. The Black Community and Brer Soul, Xeon Entertainment Group, 1971, videotape.

9. *Shaft*, dir. Gordon Parks Sr., 98 min., Metro-Goldwyn-Mayer, Starring Richard Roundtree and Moses Gunn.

10. Quentin Tarantino and Jackie Brown will be discussed further in the next section.

11. Bob Thompson, "The Shaft Attitude Cool Dude Samuel L. Jackson is 'Looking Good and Being Bad,'" *Toronto Sun*, 11 June 2000, p. S3.

12. Thompson, "The Shaft Attitude," 53.

13. *Superfly*, dir. Gordon Parks Jr., 93 min., Warner Brothers, 1972. Starring Ron O'Neal, Carl Lee, Julius Harris, Sheila Frazier and Charles McGregor.

14. Ibid.

15. As quoted in Bogle, *Toms, Coons, Mulattoes, Mammies*, 430.

16. Bogle, 431.

17. Ibid., 428.

18. *I Got the Hook Up*, dir. Michael Martin, 93 min., Dimension Films. Starring Master P and A.J. Johnson.

19. *Belly*, dir. Hype Williams, 95 min. Artisan International, 1998. Starring Nas, DMX, Taral Hicks, Tionne 'T-Boz' Watkins, Method Man, and Tryin Turner.

20. *The Long Kiss Goodnight*, dir. Rennie Harlin, 111 min., New Line Cinema, 1997.

21. Ibid.

22. *Sneakers*, dir. Phil Alden Robinson, 125 min., Universal Studios, 1992.

23. Ibid.

24. Ibid.

25. Ibid.

26. *Men In Black*, dir. Barry Sonnenfeld, 98 min., Columbia Pictures, 1997.

27. Ibid.

28. Ibid.

29. Ibid.

30. Ibid.

31. Robert M. Entman and Andrew Rojecki. *The Black Image in the White Mind* (Chicago: University of Chicago Press, 2000), 201.

6

Modern-Day "Blaxploitation": Gangsta Rap and Its Perpetuation of the Black Demon Stereotype

I had a discussion with a few rappers a while back, and I asked them why they use so much profanity and are so misogynistic in their music.

"Rev, we're like a mirror to society," one of the rappers said. "We are merely reflecting what we see."

"Well, I don't know about you, but I use a mirror to correct what's wrong with me," I told them. "I don't look in the mirror to see my hair messed up and my teeth need brushing and just walk out of the house that way. I use the mirror to fix me."

This hip-hop culture must use their music, their influence to correct what's wrong, not to continue to perpetuate what's wrong, not continue to promote what's wrong. They have the power to do that. And if they really want to have an impact on society, they must change their focus and show America the best of us instead of the worst.[1]

As discussed in chapter 2, historically, colonialist imperatives have chosen to deem those of African descent to be hypersexual and violent. This stereotype is upheld by the "gangsta's" railing against bitches and "hos," his glorification of violence, and his embrace of capitalist greed[2]—oftentimes simultaneously.[3] Rap began around 1975 when disc jockeys (DJs) brought turntables and soul and funk records to block parties, manipulating original music to create continuous beats. Lyricists soon stepped in, borrowing from Jamaican "toasting"—catchy rhyming over a beat. Its early commercial success came five years later, with the Sugarhill Gang's "Rapper's Delight" became the form's first Billboard hit. The song displayed rap's essential attributes—nimble wordplay and a danceable, funky rhythm.[4] For the next two decades, politically outspoken rappers such as Public Enemy, with their challenging lyrics about equality and police brutality, still seized the headlines, but less in-your-face artists such as MC Hammer, Will Smith, and Vanilla Ice (one of the first white rappers) capitalized on the appeal of irresistible beats.[5] But things would soon change in the 1990s. Rap music became the only genre in the history of American entertainment that is populated by such criminal types that fights have broken out at music awards ceremonies, editors have been threatened by members of groups because their magazines have not written about them and, in the most startling examples of the perplexing lines between violent fantasies and reality, big-time rap stars have been shot down. Rap music gained a violent reputation in the 1990s, when gangsta rappers began making millions performing rhymes about killing people (especially the police).[6] Although there is no empirical evidence that suggests that gangsta rap music causes violence, it is the contention of the present study that gangsta rap music certainly perpetuates the stereotype of the African American male criminal. In fact, some leaders maintain that gangsta rap music is promoting crime by influencing juvenile muggers by aggrandizing fashion labels and designers' clothes, trainers, jewelry and mobile phones. "It is though there is a juvenile competition and a feeling that you don't look the part without a lot of these accoutrements," and as a result youngsters are turning to vicious street crime to obtain them.[7] Moreover, the Reverend Paul Scott started a boycott asking people to refrain from buying compact discs that disrespect women, glorify violence, or otherwise denigrate black people. Hedonism, self-hate, and misogyny are often found in gangsta rap lyrics. Many songs glorify the prison culture, the pimp culture, and the drug culture. There is also a great deal of conspicuous consumption promoted in gangsta rap lyrics as well as in the attire they wear; the latest example includes charm bracelets. Some rappers are reported as paying as much as $11,000 for custom-made charm bracelets. Among the most prominent rap artists who have infiltrated the fashion world with their own flashy clothing collections are Eminem, Beyonce, 50 Cent, Nelly, Puff Daddy and Jay-Z.

One of the intriguing elements of the gangsta rap success story has been the mind-set of the fans who consume the music. In a survey conducted in September 2000, over 1,200 people were surveyed about their attitudes regarding rap music. Of these respondents, forty-one percent reported that they listen to rap music. According to *Source* magazine, as many as seventy-five percent of rap compact diskettes are bought by young white males, most of those males suburban.[8] One may venture to guess that the contact many of these white males have with African Americans is very minimal, hence, suggesting that the negative images presented in the compact diskettes they are purchasing is the only glimpse they have into the African American community.

As the figures in table 6.1 show, in a survey about attitudes regarding rap music, when asked whether they thought that rap contains too much violence, sixty-four percent of the respondents answered yes, and when asked whether they thought rap contains too much sex, fifty-nine percent of the respondents answered yes. Would these suburban, white, young males purchase these compact diskettes if the rap artists were to describe violence in white communities? And what if the artists referred to young white females as "bitches" and "hos?" I doubt if the present demographic would flock to the stores to purchase such CDs—especially in light of the fact that fifty-eight percent of these respondents answered "yes" when asked whether rap music has a bad attitude toward women. Consider the lyrics of "Down Ass Bitch," by popular rap artist Ja Rule:

> If you'd lie for me, like you lovin me
> Baby say yeah
> If you'd die for me, like you cry for me,
> Baby say yeah
> If you'd kill for me, like you comfort me,
> Baby say yeah,
> Girl I'm convinced, you're my down ass bitch[9]

"There's a trend now in rap to talk about the 'ride-or-die chick,'—a girl who will do anything for her man," said Pough. "That music can create a mind-set for some people. And right now, there is a growing prison population of women in jail for their relationships, in jail for selling drugs and committing crimes for their boyfriends."[10] Hence, similar to the embracing of the early caricatures of blacks in film, today's white youth have caricaturized the gangsta rapper as a black demon and finds much entertainment with its new pet. Moreover, because misogyny upholds patriarchal values and stereotypes of African Americans, and is thus comprehensible to young, middle-class, white suburban males, white kids can rebel against their parents by appropriating this art form's discourse without actually understanding social stratification and without calling into question capitalist patriarchal values.[11]

If whites are exploiting the criminal images in gangsta rap music, why is it that African Americans are writing the lyrics and creating the fashions? Two

Table 6.1
Gangsta Rap/Hip Hop Survey

Do you personally ever listen to rap or hip hop music?

Yes	No	Don't Know
41%	56%	3%

(I'm going to read you some different forms of popular entertainment. As I read each one, please tell me whether you think it contains too much violence or if you think this is generally not a problem.) Do you think this contains too much violence or is it generally not a problem? Rap or hip hop music?

Too Much	Not a Problem	Don't Know
64%	22%	14%

(As I read the list once more, this time please tell me whether you think each of the following contains too much sex or if you think this is generally not a problem.) Do you think this contains too much sex or is it generally not a problem? Rap or hip hop music?

Too Much	Not a Problem	Don't Know
59%	24%	17%

Do you think rap music . . . is less political than it used to be?

Yes	No	Don't Know
35%	29%	36%

Do you think rap music . . . has a bad attitude toward women?

Yes	No	Don't Know
58%	21%	21%

(Now, thinking just about the past 10 years or so, I'm going to read another list of changes that have taken place. Please tell me if you think each one has been a change for the better, a change for the worse, or hasn't made much difference.) Has . . . rap music . . . been a change for the better, a change for the worse, or hasn't made much difference?[1]

Change for the Better	Change for the Worse	Hasn't Made Much Difference	Don't Know/Refused
14%	53%	26%	7%

(Please tell me how much—if at all—you or other members of your family are influenced by rap or hip hop music.) In your family, how much does hip hop music influence . . . attitudes toward women and violence . . . a lot, somewhat, only a little, or not at all?

A lot	Somewhat	Only a Little	Not at all[2]
11%	5%	7%	71%

(Please tell me how much—if at all—you or other members of your family are influenced by rap or hip hop music.) In your family, how much does hip hop music influence . . . speech—a lot, somewhat, only a little, or not at all?

A lot	Somewhat	Only a Little	Not at all[3]
7%	8%	11%	69%

Please tell me how much—if at all—you or other members of your family are influenced by rap or hip hop music. In your family, how much does hip hop music influence . . . dress—a lot, somewhat, only a little, or not at all?

A lot	Somewhat	Only a Little	Not at all[4]
8%	8%	10%	69%

This telephone survey was conducted by Princeton Survey Research Associates for *Newsweek* from September 27–29, 2000. The population was taken from a national sample of adults (respondents are 18 or older). Unless otherwise noted, the number of participants was 1,231.

1. Number of participants for this question is 1, 546.

2. Don't Know = 6%.

3. Don't Know = 5%.

4. Don't Know = 5%

reasons: money and the fact that many gangsta rappers lead very violent lifestyles. The careers of Ice-T, NWA (Niggaz With Attitude), Suge Knight, Tupac Shakur, Puff Daddy (or P. Diddy), and Snoop Dogg will be discussed to illustrate these very important points.

ICE-T

It is ironic that the rapper who released the song "Cop Killer" is now playing a detective on the National Broadcasting Company's (NBC's) *Law and Order: Special Victim's Unit*. Ice-T (born Tracy Marrow) was orphaned at a young age, spent many years in a Los Angeles street gang, and served in the U.S. Army's elite Rangers force. Somehow, these experiences gave him his distinct style of rage and alienation. In 1991, Ice-T landed a leading role in *New Jack City* (1991), a film very similar to *Superfly* (1972) in that the main characters were not presented as mere drug dealers, but as businessmen drug dealers who were not only street-smart but lived very extravagant lifestyles. Since *New Jack City*, Ice-T has appeared in more than two dozen films, produced other acts, and written a best-selling book entitled *The Ice Opinion*. Ice-T is presently working on another album with a group called SMG (Sex, Money and Guns). He describes this album as very hard core and very gangsta— further perpetuating the black demon stereotype.

NWA

NWA (Niggaz With Attitude) was a group of high school dropouts who pretended to be racist gangsters, dope dealers, cop killers, rapists, and murderous thugs. Their music glorified bombings and drive-by shootings—in short, their music did absolutely nothing to encourage or positively empower African American youth. Once, during a performance, they told their audience, "You're either down for whatever, or you're a punk-ass bitch." The clear message in NWA's music was, "The world owes us a comfortable living because we're black—get your money any way that you can." Their music videos depicted the group members as slaves picking cotton, their "master" portrayed as a Los Angeles policeman riding a horse and carrying a shotgun.[12] Jeff Liles maintains:

[E]very time a Roots, Common, Nina Simone, Erykah Badu or D'Angelo gifts us with an important message of inspiration, hope, preservation or love, another African American recording artist (or 10) immediately steps up and reinforces the hideous negative "gangsta" stereotype, packaging racial/urban distress as "entertainment," then selling it back to an eager, predominantly white audience. . . . Public Enemy was militant and educated; the members of NWA were merely anti-social role players and their music was prostitution on a number of different levels. It sold out the urban African-American public as a people who justified violent crime as a reasonable means to an end. At the same time, they (along with Ice-T and, later, Tupac Shakur) allowed white entertainment executives to pimp them out as ideological spokesmen for their fractured and desperate community.[13]

The members of NWA often said that their music was not manufactured, but merely a slice of their normal everyday lives. This is not true; members of the band—Dr. Dre, MC Ren, Ice Cube and DJ Yella—were never Los Angeles gang members. They never killed a policeman during a drive-by shooting and, in fact, only Eazy-E ever actually stood on a Compton street corner and sold crack cocaine. And interestingly enough, Eazy-E contributed $1,000 to George Bush's presidential campaign in 1992 and when Eazy-E died from complications of the HIV virus in 1995, he left behind seven children by six different women. Also worth noting is the fact that Dr. Dre once severely beat up a female reporter in public and Ice Cube gave up an academic scholarship to Arizona State to remain a part of NWA, which came at a great price—his mother's house was the target of a number of drive-by shootings by real gang members. According to Liles, it is fair to surmise that the only motivation for any member of NWA during their popularity was the accumulation of money. They were, in fact, capitalist businessmen whose product was a depiction of the degradation and isolation of the collective African American community—a problem they actually contributed to, rather than helped to rectify.[14]

TUPAC SHAKUR

On September 8, 1996, Tupac Shakur, one of the most controversial and commercially successful rap stars, was shot as he sat in a black BMW 750 sedan, waiting at a traffic light in Las Vegas, Nevada. He was twenty-five years old. Shakur's childhood was pretty traumatic. He was born Lesane Crooks to Afeni Shakur, who was a crack-smoking member of the New Black Panthers. Shakur spent his early childhood in New York before moving to Baltimore, where he enrolled in the prestigious Baltimore School for the Arts. He was considered to be a "natural performer."[15] The Baltimore School for the Arts was not enough to prevent Tupac from being involved in drug offenses and acts of violence including shootings and even sexual assault. Eventually, Shakur signed with Death

Row Records and sold millions of records. He also starred in several films, including *Juice* (1992), *Poetic Justice* (1993), and *Gridlock'd* (1997).

Death Row Records is owned by Marion (Suge) Knight, a multimillionaire who has been incarcerated in a California prison for nearly five years. Knight is a very controversial figure in that he is alleged to be connected to the Bloods, one of Los Angeles' most feared black gangs. Knight is said to run his empire by bullying and violence. In the words of former Los Angeles Police Department detective Russell Poole, "Knight was one of the most powerful gangsters around. He was well organized; he had a lot of power and kept dozens of police officers working in his organization."[16]

For Shakur, Knight was "the father-figure protector" he always wanted and the two men socialized together, beat people up together, and started a feud with Bad Boy Records operated by Sean (Puffy) Combs. According to police reports, Knight had a friend or nephew who was shot in Atlanta; he blamed Puffy Combs and the feud began.[17] Then in November 1994, while awaiting a verdict after being charged with raping a fan, Shakur was shot in the head, hand, and groin by someone he believed to be an associate of Puffy Combs. Having recovered from his wounds, Shakur was jailed for four-and-a-half years for sexual touching without consent but released after Knight paid for a bond. While in jail, Shakur had been told by a fellow inmate that Biggie Smalls (another gangsta rapper and one-time friend of Shakur) had been behind his shooting, although Smalls had always denied it. Knight, meanwhile, used a televised black music award ceremony to declare war on Puff Daddy, as Combs was also known, and Bad Boy Records. Meanwhile, Shakur emerged from jail in October 1995 and threw himself into his work. By early 1996, he was dating Kikada Jones, daughter of legendary composer and producer Quincy Jones. He also began to look for ways of escaping from Knight, because he had become convinced that Death Row Records had stolen from his earnings. According to David Thomas, Knight owed Shakur millions and Shakur was about to leave Death Row Records and do an audit.[18] Another former Los Angeles officer who worked off-duty for Knight reported that he had heard "heated money" disputes between Shakur and Knight, that Shakur was owed at least twent million dollars, and that he was planning to leave Death Row Records. Early in September, Shakur was still a Death Row artist when he was invited to a Mike Tyson fight in Las Vegas by Knight. While there, Shakur was involved in an assault on another young black man, Orlando Anderson. After he was told that Anderson was a member of the Crips—rivals of Knight's gang, the Bloods, who had stolen a medallion belonging to Death Row—Shakur attacked Anderson and Knight joined in, kicking Anderson as he lay on the floor. Shortly after eleven o'clock that night, a white Cadillac with California license plates drew up alongside the BMW in which Knight and Shakur were sitting. A black man got out and fired thirteen shots into the BMW. Shakur was fatally wounded; Knight, on the other hand, claimed to have been hit in the head by a bullet. In fact, he escaped with no more than a scratch from flying glass. The last years of Shakur's life, even after he became a star, were a continual round of arrests, court appearances, and jail sentences.

SUGE KNIGHT

Marion (Suge) Knight entered the music business in 1988 after attending the University of Nevada at Las Vegas with a major in business. Knight tried out for the Los Angeles Rams but did not make the cut, so he decided to become a celebrity bodyguard, eventually working for rhythm-and-blues singer Bobby Brown. According to some sources, Knight received his gangsta reputation in 1991 when he helped a producer friend who had worked with Vanilla Ice on his album "Ice, Ice Baby." Vanilla Ice, a white rapper, had allegedly failed to pay the producer royalties and it is reported that Knight paid the young star a visit and allegedly dangled him from a hotel balcony. Knight walked away with the publishing rights to Vanilla Ice's album.[19] Knight's next break came when he befriended Dr. Dre, a member of the seminal gangsta rap group NWA and convinced him to go solo. After putting up $100,000 of his own money, Knight approached Jimmy Iovine and Ted Fields of Interscope Records, which at the time was a struggling label owned by Time Warner. Iovine and Fields signed Knight and Dr. Dre and the subsequent album sold over five million copies.[20] Under Knight's watch, threats, beat-downs, and gunplay were commonplace. In 1993, the FBI launched an investigation into alleged money laundering, drug trafficking and gang activity at the label. In 1994, Knight was convicted of beating two musicians at a Death Row studio with a telephone. At one Death Row party in April 1995, a young man was beaten to death; no one was arrested. Later that year, however, at a company Christmas party in Beverly Hills, Knight allegedly forced a music producer to drink urine from a champagne glass after the man refused to give him the address of the mother of Puffy Combs who, as president of the New York–based Bad Boy Records, was Knight's biggest rival.[21] Allison Samuels writes:

Even in prison, Knight kept getting into trouble. A year-and-a-half into his sentence, he became a subject in the investigation of the March 1997 murder of rapper Christopher (Notorious BIG, also known as Biggie Smalls) Wallace, the most successful act on Puffy Combs' label. Though a getaway car linked to the murder was found at one of Knight's houses, the investigation was dropped for lack of evidence.[22]

P. DIDDY

By many accounts, Sean (Puffy) Combs (now known as P. Diddy) is the conservative American Dream: a middle-class businessman and a corporate success story. Puff Daddy (an alternate name Combs used) associated with models, sports stars, and movie stars, and was once engaged to actress and singer Jennifer Lopez. Puffy first entered the music industry when, at the age of 18, he secured a work placement at Uptown, a rap label. He was very successful as a manager and eventually dropped out of college to work there full time. His big break came when he spotted Biggie, a 19-year-old from Brooklyn, and at that point he started Bad Boy as a label within Uptown before leaving Uptown but not without taking his protégé with him. Combs and Biggie worked together to make the Notorious BIG's debut album, "Ready to Die," that went double platinum, but it also brought about a mini-war in the gangsta rap community. Like the turf wars of the street gangs that many of the artists had grown up with, it was all about territory. On the one hand were the West Coast rappers of California led by Tupac Shakur; on the other were the East Coast Bad Boys, whose figurehead was Smalls and whose mentor was Puff Daddy. Throughout the early 1990s, the war escalated until, in 1997, Smalls was gunned down shortly after leaving a Los Angeles party with Combs. The murder was a direct retaliation for the killing of Shakur, and Smalls was rumored to have been involved. Biggie Smalls' death made Puff Daddy a household name in that his "tribute" to his dead friend, "I'll Be Missing You," hit number one. Puff Daddy sold twelve million albums in three years and earned approximately thirty million dollars a year. In April 1999, after an argument with Steven Stoute of Interscope records, he entered Stoute's office with his bodyguards and beat him up. He escaped a prison stretch only with a public apology, a one million-dollar payout, and a guilty plea to the lesser crime of harassment violation. Later that year, on Christmas at Club New York, a dispute started involving Combs when he shoved someone, spilling his drink. The man taunted Combs about his multimillion-dollar income, accusing him of losing credibility. After some arguing, about $3,000 was thrown at Combs as an insult. As people in the club tried to grab the money, Combs and members of his entourage drew pistols and opened fire. Combs later was charged with bribery when it was alleged that Combs offered his chauffeur $35,000 to say that the gun that was found in Combs's car was his, an illegal gun possession.

A history of guns, violence, and ostentatious displays of wealth have punctuated Puff Daddy's rise to a one-man entertainment empire as chief executive of Bad Boy—originally a record company but now including film and TV companies, a clothing range, restaurants, recording studios, and publishing firms—as well as a resident of the swanky Hamptons and cover star of Forbes and GQ magazines:

Combs has always been obsessed with the glamorous, macho world of "gangstas"—the rapper's adaptation of gangsters—but this time the obsession that has made him one of the most powerful black men in America could be the very thing that finishes him off. Because, despite the guns and gold and gangsta protestations, he is no bad boy made good. Puff Daddy is no ghetto kid rapping his way out of the gutter. He was a polite, middle-class boy from a well-to-do part of Harlem and a former model for Baskin-Robbins ice cream. He went to a private Catholic boys' school and studied business in college. He got good grades ("I was scared to death to bring home any grade below a B") and was a regular for the school football and baseball teams.[23]

SNOOP DOGG

The person who most personifies the pimp from the blaxploitation era is Snoop Dogg, born Calvin Broadus. Snoop was incarcerated shortly after he finished high school for selling crack, and has admitted to his association with the Los Angeles gang, the Crips. In 1993, he was found not guilty for the shooting death of Philip Woldermariam by his bodyguard McKinley Lee. The braided and goateed performer has dominated gangsta rap music with chart toppers such as "Doggystyle," "No Limit Top Dogg," and "Tha Last Meal." All in all, Snoop has sold over fourteen million records in the United States but, like many gangsta rappers, has an ongoing feud with Marion "Suge" Knight that has been going on ever since Snoop left Death Row Records in 1998. Since 1998, Snoop has been on Priority Records, a well-known rap label owned by EMI Group PLC. The label has gone through steep cutbacks and recently was absorbed into the company's Capitol Records label. Also recently, Snoop signed with MCA, a unit of Vivendi Universal SA, which gives him his own label—Doggystyle Records—and budget for developing new artists, whose recordings he will own. Snoop has access to the marketing, promotion, and distribution channels of Universal, the industry's market-share leader.

Snoop has teamed up with pornography king Larry Flint and produced a number of pornographic videos entitled, *Snoop Dogg's Doggystyle*. He has received additional backers in this venture, including from Hustler Video, and MCA plans to distribute less racy videos by Snoop's Snoopadelic Films. Beyond that, he is auditioning for roles in feature films. So far, Snoop's movie work has received mixed reviews. He was praised for a chilling performance as an ex-con in 2000's *Baby Boy* and as a wheelchair-bound drug dealer in the Academy Award–winning film *Training Day* (2001). But when he starred as a vengeance-seeking ghost pimp in *Bones* (2001), the film bombed. Among his most profitable cinematic ventures to date is Snoop Dogg's *Doggystyle*, winner of several adult-film industry awards. In that movie, shot at his home, Snoop narrates as actors have sex. The scenes are intermingled with new Snoop Dogg music videos, which expose his music to a new audience.

Pimp references have been an element of Snoop's projects; he actually did some pimping for a while, but has given it up. In recent years, the imagery that surrounds soliciting business for prostitutes—long mink coats, coordinated satin suits and scantily clad women—has become a staple of his blaxploitation moniker; he recently purchased a "Snoop DeVille," a customized "pimpmobile," with multiple TV screens and seats lined in mink. Another symbol of the pimp image: personalized, rhinestone-encrusted goblets that he drinks from in all public appearances. Like most successful gangsta rappers, Snoop works with a small team of advisors. Stephen Barnes, his lawyer, handles the bulk of his business negotiations, which have helped Snoop land a steady stream of movie parts and product endorsements for Nike and XM Satellite Radio, among others. Also guiding Snoop is the actual "retired" pimp, Bishop Don Magic Juan, who says he gave up pimping years ago when he became a Christian, is part spiritual guide, part cheerleader, and part accessory for Snoop as he adopts the pimp esthetic.

Because of Snoop Dogg's success in the pornography business[24] other gangsta rap artists are following suit: 50 Cent has brokered a deal with a company called Digital Sin and will release an interactive sex DVD titled "Groupie Luv" later this year. Rappers Lil John and the East Side Boyz released "Lil John and the East Side Boyz American Sex Series" in February 2004. And as of January 2004, Playboy TV introduced a new hip-hop-themed series called "Buckwild" where rap stars like OutKast, Snoop Dogg, Nelly and Busta Rhymes horse around with a troupe of women called the Buckwild Girls, who seem to fall out of their clothes whenever a camera approaches.

One cannot ignore that gangsta rap arose specifically not to gratify mass-cultural channels and dominant perceptions; instead, it has played a major role in the pandering of materialism, violence, and especially misogyny; the present discourse turns in its criticism to the media itself. In addition to blatantly taking to their logical extremes the dictates of American patriarchy, gangsta rap in effect throws the system in the system's face: it wins the game by playing by the very rules that are in place. Thus, misogyny can be satirical and paradoxical—it both allows the rapper to reap the benefits of the capitalist system and serves as scapegoat for the agents of social control or conservative powers that be. Gangsta rap does not threaten patriarchal or capitalist order but, at the same time, it could be said to unabashedly mock those same imperatives. In a way, it serves everyone's purposes—except those of women.

NOTES

1. Reverend Al Sharpton, "The Hip Hop Generation," Electronic Urban Report, retrieved 2 January 2003. Available at http://eurweb.com.

2. Consider these lyrics from "The Eminem Show," for which Eminem received the best rap album award at the Grammys:

> Now I don't wanna hit no woman when this chick's got it coming
> Someone better get this bitch before she gets kicked in the stomach
> And she's pregnant, but she's egging me on, begging me to throw her
> Off the steps on this porch, my only weapon is force

As reported by Dana Williams, "Hip Hop's Bad Rap?" *Hate in the News*, retrieved 14 August 2003. "Fight Hate and Promote Tolerance," a Web project by the Southern Poverty Law Center, available at http://www.tolerance.org.

3. "Misogyny in Gangsta Rap: The Future of Radical Conservatism? Blatant Blaxploitation? A Painting of Modern Life? Or Something Else Entirely?" Retrieved August 14, 2003. Available at http://mediastudies.ponoma.edu.

4. As reported by Andrew Curry, "Rude Awakening: The Beat Goes On, Even as Rap Keeps Changing," *U.S. News and World Report* (8 July 2002), 65.

5. Jenga Mwendo, 24-year-old artistic director of "Red Clay's Catcalls," an acclaimed multimedia exhibit designed to simulate women's experiences with street harassment, says music has always been influential because it is so easy to digest. "Young people have always listened to whatever is popular and anything that comes with a harmony or a nice beat is easier for people to accept," said Mwendo. "But that's the problem—people may say, "I'm not listening to the lyrics; I just like the beat," when really those messages are sinking in whether it's consciously or subconsciously," and the problem is compounded by radio, she says. "Adults have a right to buy this music and listen to it. But children are exposed to it just by turning on the radio because so much of what's played on the radio is explicit and misogynistic." Many times, even "clean" song versions contain explicit messages. Mwendo cites West Coast rapper Nate Dogg's newest track, "I Need Me a Bitch." Changed to "I Need Me a Chick" for radio, the core of the song remains unchanged:

> I need me a chick, who ain't scared to flirt
> I need me a chick in the middle of the grocery store she'll lift up her skirt
> I need me a chick, like I need my crew
> I need me a chick to pass on to my boys soon as I get through

"You can bleep out the dirty words, but the message is still there," said Mwendo. "It's shocking. It's a message that says women are objects, that it's okay to use women and just pass them along to your boys." As reported by Dana Williams 2003, "Hip Hop's Bad Rap?" Available at http://www.tolerance.org.

6. In this chapter, I will address only the most egregious gangsta rap music. It seems as though the rap that gets the most press for its radical views is misogynistic and violent gangsta rap, whereas truly subversive, anticapitalist, pro-black rhymes are diluted or ignored by the mass media. Conservatism is upheld, and the fascination of youth and their mobile dollars is spent on upholding negative stereotypes of African Americans. The case of Digable Planets is an example with their abstract lyrics that advocate socialism and radical Black Nationalism, but as member Butler explains, "Every time we explained in an interview what the insect thing (their M.C. names) was about, which was a theory based around socialism, communism and revolution, it never made it onto the printed page." This is probably because Planets' message is more potentially dangerous than that of gangster rappers because they are offering a radical critique that goes completely against America's present economic structure, and that could end in a destruction of the system. Gangsta rappers are, after all, the consummate capitalists. And, in addition to Digable Planets—before gangsta rappers draped themselves with platinum and diamonds, before they wrote rhymes about pimping and killing, before they made videos with champagne and fancy cars—there were rappers such as Run-DMC, who rhymed about going to college and told funny tales from daily life. For the most part, their messages were positive.

7. Lord Warner, Youth Justice Board Chairman. As quoted in "Gangstas Get Rap," *Perth Sunday Times*, 21 April 2002, p. 34.

8. In fact, rap is dependent on white money—the supposedly independent label Def Jam is a subsidiary of Universal Music Group and Russell Simmons, the labels chairman, estimates that eighty percent of hip-hop's audience is white.

9. Dana Williams, http://www.tolerance.org.

10. Ibid.

11. "Misogyny in Gangsta Rap: The Future of Radical Conservatism? Blatant Blaxploitation? A Painting of Modern Life? Or Something Else Entirely?" Retrieved 8 August 2003. Available at http://www.mediastudies.pomona.edu.

12. As reported by Jeff Liles, *Dallas Observer*, 12 September 2002.

13. Liles, 38.

14. Ibid.

15. As reported by David Thomas, the "Sunday Magazine" of the *Sunday Herald Sun*, 9 June 2002, p. Z08.

16. Thomas, Z08.

17. Ibid.

18. Ibid.

19. As reported by Allison Samuels, *Newsweek*, (23 April 2001), 54.

20. Samuels, 54.

21. Ibid.

22. Ibid.

23. Dominic Utton, "As the Cult Superstar Appears in Court, We Look at How This Middle-Class Boy Could—Have Become a Victim of His Desire to Prove Himself to Fans; Is This the Rap That Will Finally Make a True Gangsta Out of Puff Daddy?" *The Express* (2001): 42.

24. In an industry where a video that sells 4,000 copies is considered a runaway hit, "Snoop Dogg's Doggystyle" sold somehwere "in the hundreds of thousands," according to Larry Flint, president of Larry Flint Publications, which owns Hustler Video. It was named top-selling tape of 2001 by the porn trade publication Adult Video News and was the first hardcore video ever listed on the Billboard music video sales chart. (As reported by Martin Edlund of the *New York Times*, March 7, 2004, available at: http:www.nytimes.com/2004/03/07/arts/music/07EDLU.html?8br.)

7

Conclusion and Suggestions for Moving Forward

It was posited in this thesis that the negative stereotypes that many people have of African American men are created to a significant degree by the mass media, and mass media particularly seems to be obsessed with the idea that there is a fundamental weakness in African American families that can be traced to their experiences as slaves. The black demon stereotype was thus created especially in connection with the inaccurate notion that African American males have a very high propensity toward wanting to rape white women. These images are especially purported by newspaper crime articles, Hollywood films, gangsta rap music, and news talk shows hosted by ultraconservative media personalities such as Rush Limbaugh, Bill O'Reilly, and Patrick Buchanan; such media have taken the lead in equating young African American males with aggressiveness, lawlessness, and violence. Hence, a historical analysis of African Americans was presented to illustrate the origin and extent to which media and personalities, as such, especially those who purport to represent America's "moral majority," have used negative stereotypes to retain African Americans as second-class citizens.

Next, the theoretical schema coined "conceptual entrapment by media imagery" was introduced to illustrate how the public conceptualizes, and consequently believes, the stereotypes depicted in the media of African American males as criminals. According to this schema, the world of crime the public believes exists is based on individual knowledge, from knowledge gained from social interactions with other people, and most important, from the knowledge they gain from mass media that ultimately provide the context for them to act in accordance with their constructed view of crime. Hence, there is a cyclical effect in constructing the concept crime in that once people perceive concepts to be real, they go out and look for examples of these concepts. Thus, a beginning to better understand crime, according to this schema, is to realize that definitions of crime are not absolute; they change over time and according to the power structure of any given society. The image of the black demon as disseminated in mass media is not coincidental, nor does it exist in a vacuum; the public demands this image by supporting it through purchasing tickets for films that portray negative images of African Americans, purchasing gangsta rap compact discs, and by not challenging the images on television, especially its news programs. (Perhaps we should rethink the entire Nielsen's ratings system.) As the public has learned violence and prejudice over the years, it too can unlearn these undesirable practices and ideals. The first step is educating the public about the consequences of such complacency toward violence and prejudice, only then will we begin to deconstruct crime, thus debunking the black demon stereotype.

IMPLICATIONS OF THE BLACK DEMON STEREOTYPE: RACIAL PROFILING

One way in which the black demon stereotype adversely affects the lives of African Americans is through racial profiling. Racial profiling is defined as the use of race as an indicator in a profile of criminal suspects. In short, drivers are being stopped either entirely or in part because of their race or ethnicity.[1] *Driving while black* (DWB) is the catch phrase being used to describe racial profiling; it is a practice that many police departments steadfastly deny, but one that many African Americans report as an ugly rite of passage for black and Latino drivers. For example, a car filled with young African American or Latino men has a good chance of being stopped. A black or Latino man or woman driving through a mostly white area can arouse suspicion, and if they are driving a nice car, there is a good chance that they will be pulled over. In the nation's long-drawn-out and too often ill-advised "war on drugs," U.S. highways have become like minefields for motorists of color as authorities comb the roads in search of mules—those smuggling narcotics—and, often, guns. Without warning, an innocent black driver can end up parked on a highway shoulder, face to face with the law. Sometimes, motorists are ticketed for minor infractions, such as a cracked taillight or making an illegal lane change. But the main purpose of their stop is to be questioned, and often have their vehicles and belongings searched. Then they are sent on their way, many times without an explanation or apology.

According to one African American police officer who works in Dade County, Florida, ninety percent of the people they stop have their rights infringed on and are humiliated. This same police officer was pulled over himself early one evening while driving to a house he was building in North Florida.[2] The incident, caught on videotape and now part of the officer's own efforts to expose what he calls a "racist game of smoke and mirrors," ended in a scuffle with Orange County deputies. The African American officer was pepper sprayed and arrested. He says he has spent nearly $100,000 fighting the case. He was found guilty of a misdemeanor and has a civil suit pending; he says:

The intent is good, but the way it's being practiced by racist police officers is an abuse of power. . . . Black and Latino drivers are innocent people who haven't done anything. That's what's so bad about it. The majority of the people they are searching and humiliating are black people. That's why I was so angry. I went from being an ordinary citizen and decorated officer to a criminal in a matter of minutes.[3]

It may have taken minutes for this officer to be transformed from a law-abiding police officer to a black demon, but it has taken years for the complaints about racial profiling to make it across America's great racial divide. Finally, after years of studies and lawsuits from angry black motorists, and police denials and charges that accusations were isolated incidents or inflammatory exaggerations, the issue is getting an unprecedented level of attention across the country. In April 1999, North Carolina's governor, Jim Hunt, signed into law Senate Bill 76, which requires state law-enforcement officers to record the race, age, and gender of every motorist stopped. North Carolina, which had been sued by black motorists, was the first state to pass such legislation. Similar bills challenging racial profiling have been introduced in Congress and at least twelve other states, including those along the Interstate 95 corridor, which authorities target for heavy drug trafficking.

Former Attorney General Janet Reno, during a speech in Washington, D.C. in spring 1999, said that collecting data is necessary so we can see where the problems exist and how extensive they are. She praised the San Diego police department for its announcement of plans to voluntarily collect the information. San Jose, California also announced that it would collect data. Since Reno's presentation, the report by the San Jose police department found that Latinos

represented forty-three percent of all drivers stopped, but only thirty-one percent of the white San Jose population. These data clearly indicate a disparity in
the percentage of Latinos stopped by the police.

Along the New Jersey Turnpike, African Americans made up 13.5 percent
of the traffic and fifteen percent of the speeders, but were forty-six percent of
those pulled over. According to the Attorney General's report, arrest data from
the Computerized Criminal History database shows that from 1996 through
1998, for Cranbury, Morrestown, and Newark—the three New Jersey trooper
stations along the Turnpike—of 2,871 arrests, 61.7 percent were black and
32.5 percent were white. Five percent were other races.[4] In Florida, the *Orlando Sentinel* videotaped traffic stops and found that seventy percent of those
stopped on Interstate 95 were black motorists, even though they made up less
than ten percent of the driver population.

In Maryland, the numbers are equally disturbing, showing that whereas
17.5 percent of the traffic violators on I-95 just north of Baltimore were
African American, seventy percent of those searched by the Maryland state
police were black.[5] Note the following case. Harvard-trained lawyer Robert L.
Wilkins and several members of his family were pulled over on I-95. Wilkins,
a public defender in Washington, D.C., was returning from a funeral in
Chicago in May 1992 when the rented Cadillac he and his family were in was
stopped for speeding in western Maryland. Troopers said that the car was trav-
eling sixty miles an hour in a forty-mile-an-hour zone. The trooper ordered
Wilkins, his aunt, uncle, and cousin out of the car. Wilkins reported:

I remember standing in the rain with that German shepherd jumping all over the car
and police standing around and all the cars driving past and the occupants looking at
the dogs and the cars and us. And I remember seeing this young boy who was white,
who was in one of those cars. He was about 6 and had his face pressed against the
window the way kids do. I couldn't help but to think what that image subconsciously
told him as he is growing up. What did it help to contribute about his view of black
people? Whether it's going to contribute to him believing racist stereotypes about
blacks, or an unwarranted fear about black men.[6]

Other egregious cases of driving while black include:

• In California, San Diego Chargers football player Shawn Lee was pulled over and he
  and his girlfriend were handcuffed and detained by police for thirty minutes along Interstate 15. The officer said Lee was stopped because he was driving a vehicle that fit
  the description of one stolen that evening. But Lee was driving a Jeep Cherokee, a
  sport utility vehicle, and the reportedly stolen vehicle was a Honda sedan.[7]

- In Santa Monica, California police officers in two cruisers followed George Washington and Darryl Hicks, both African American men, as they drove into the parking garage of the hotel where they were staying. The men were ordered out of the car at gunpoint, handcuffed, and placed in separate police cars while the officers searched their car and checked their identification. The police justified this detention because the men allegedly resembled a description of two suspects being sought for 19 armed robberies and one of the men seemed to be nervous. The men filed suit against the officers and the court found that neither man fit the descriptions of the robbers and that the robberies had not even occurred in the city of Santa Monica.[8]

- A young Liberian attending college in North Carolina was driving along I-95 in Maryland when he was pulled over by state police who said he was not wearing a seatbelt. The officers detained him and his two passengers for two hours as they searched the car for illegal drugs, weapons, or other contraband. Finding nothing, they proceeded to dismantle the car and removed part of the sunroof. Again finding nothing, the officers in the end handed the young Liberian a screwdriver, saying "You're going to need this" as they left the scene."[9]

- In Indiana, an African American state police officer was pulled over while driving an unmarked car in the city of Carmel. The African American officer was wearing a uniform at the time, but he was not wearing a hat, which would have identified him as a police officer. According to a complaint filed with the American Civil Liberties Union, the white trooper appeared to be "shocked and surprised" when the African American officer in the unmarked car got out of the car. The white trooper explained that he had stopped the black officer because he had three antennas on the rear of his car and quickly left the scene.[10]

- In Pennsylvania, an African American male was pulled over while driving his cousin's Jaguar at two A.M. Five Brentwood police cars arrived on the scene. One of the officers said that the suspect ran three red lights before stopping after the officer flashed his lights at him. The officer ordered the suspect out of the car and saw him reach for something believed to be a weapon. In reality, it was a cellular phone. The officer knocked the phone out of the suspect's hand and a scuffle followed. The other officers beat the suspect with a flashlight, a collapsible baton, and a blackjack as one put his foot on the suspect's neck. The suspect, who was unarmed, died handcuffed, ankles bound, facedown on the pavement shortly after the incident began.[11]

The Bureau of Justice Statistics offers similar findings. African American drivers are stopped more often than white drivers (12.3 percent and 10.4 percent, respectively). The racial differences are even more pronounced with regard to more specific traffic-stop practices. Twice as many African American drivers as white drivers reported being stopped five or more times (3.4 percent compared with 1.6 percent). This clearly suggests that some African American drivers are being targeted by police. Whites were more likely to be stopped for speeding and drunk driving, whereas African Americans and Latinos were more likely to be stopped for vehicle defects and record checks. In addition, African American and Latino drivers were somewhat more likely to be ticketed than whites and both African Americans and Latinos were twice as likely as whites to have force used against them in a traffic stop.[12]

Harvard law professor Randall Kennedy argues that race should never be used as the basis for a police action "except in the most extraordinary of circumstances." First, if the practice is strictly forbidden, it will reduce the opportunity for the police to engage in harassment under the cloak of "reasonable" law-enforcement measures. Second, the current practice of using race "nourishes powerful feelings of racial grievance against law-enforcement authorities." Third, the resulting hostility to the police creates barriers to police—citizen cooperation in those communities "most need of police protection." Fourth, permitting the practice contributes to racial segregation, because African Americans will be reluctant to venture into white neighborhoods for fear of being stopped by the police.[13]

As a result of the black demon stereotype, racial profiling has caused much fear in African American males who are pulled over by the police, so much so that the American Civil Liberties Union has drafted pointers for African American males who are stopped by the police:

1. Stay calm and in control of your words, body language, and emotions;
2. Do not argue with officers;
3. Keep your hands in view at all times;
4. Don't run;
5. Don't resist even if you are innocent;
6. Don't complain on the scene or tell the police they're wrong or that you're going to file a complaint;
7. Do not make any statements regarding the incident;
8. Ask for a lawyer immediately if you're arrested;
9. Remember the officers' badge patrol car numbers;
10. Immediately write down everything you remember;
11. Try to find witnesses and get their names and telephone numbers;
12. If you feel your rights have been violated, file a written complaint with the police department's internal affairs division or civilian complaint board.[14]

Driving while black is just one example of the numerous negative effects that the media's proliferation of the black demon has had on this society. Police use of excessive force is another way in which the media's perpetuation of this

stereotype has manifested itself. Because the police are the symbolic representatives of the established order, incidents of excessive force are perceived as part
of the broader patterns of equality and discrimination in society.

SUGGESTIONS

One of the first things we must do is teach history the way it really happened and not sugar coat certain atrocities such as slavery and the Holocaust.
We cannot fully comprehend our present condition without accurately understanding our past. I recently took an undergraduate seminar to visit the
Bell Meade Plantation in Nashville, Tennessee. During the tour of the plantation and slave quarters, the tour guide referred to slaves as "laborers."
When questioned by students in the seminar about why she used the "laborers" label, she responded that the term "slave" was much too harsh and that
the Bell Meade Plantation was a good plantation for African American
slaves. Her reasoning is similar to a medical doctor diagnosing a patient as
having "good cancer!" How ridiculous!

Another thing we must do is diversify our newsrooms. An annual national
survey of newsroom personnel reports that the percentage of minorities in
television newsrooms nationwide has dropped from twenty-five percent to
eighteen percent; this compares with minorities' roughly thirty percent share
of the U.S. population.[15] The survey also found that minority television
news directors fell to 6.6 percent from 9.2 percent a year ago. The number of
minorities in television news actually increased, but not as quickly as overall
staff rose. In radio, the minority workforce represented 6.5 percent in 2003,
down from eight percent in 2002. The proportion of minority radio news directors inched down to five percent from 5.1 percent. The proportion of
blacks in television news has fallen steadily over the past decade, from 10.1
percent in 1994 to 8.4 percent in 2003. In radio, blacks represent 4.8 percent of the workforce, up from 4.1 percent last year but down from 5.7 percent in 1994. Blacks fare even worse in broadcast news management,
representing only 0.9 percent of TV news directors and 2.5 percent of radio
news directors. In 1994, 1.6 percent of TV news directors and 5.4 percent of
radio news directors were black, according to the annual survey.

Another way to bury the black demon stereotype is to convince Hollywood
that the public will pay to see decent, humane black films; and what should
the role of the black artist be in all of this? Bogle suggests it best:

If there are to be significant African American films, the black actors, the directors,
the writers, the producers, and the technicians who are now being given the chance to

work must articulate the contemporary African American mind, his/her point of view, aspirations, and goals. The black filmmaker must come to terms with the world in which he or she lives, whether it be across 125th Street or an integrated suburb that is perhaps nothing more than a prison. African American films can liberate audiences from illusions, black and white, and in so freeing can give all of us vision and truth. It is a tremendous responsibility, much greater than that placed on ordinary white moviemakers. But the dignity of the African American man and woman has traditionally lain in his or her ability to face reality no matter how senseless it may seem and then, if lucky, to alter that reality.[16]

NOTES

1. Samuel Walker, Cassia Spohn, Miriam DeLone. *The Color of Justice: Race, Ethnicity and Crime in America*, 3rd ed. (Belmont, CA: Wadsworth/Thomson, 2004), 111.

2. As reported by Marcia Davis, "Traffic Violation: Racial Profiling Is a Reality for Black Drivers," *Emerge* (June 1999), 42.

3. Davis, "Traffic violation," 42.

4. David Harris. *Profiles in Injustice: Why Racial Profiling Doesn't Work* (New York: New Press, 2002).

5. Harris, *Profiles in Injustice*, 68.

6. As reported by Davis, "Traffic Violations," 42.

7. As reported in the *San Diego Union-Tribune*, 13 December 1997.

8. As reported in the *Los Angeles Times*, 6 November 1996.

9. As reported in Raleigh, North Carolina, the *News and Observer*, 11 June 1998.

10. As reported in the *Indianapolis Star*, 29 January 1997.

11. As reported in *People*, (15 January 1996).

12. United States Bureau of Justice Statistics. *Contacts between Police and the Public: Findings from the 1999 National Survey* (Washington, DC: U.S. Government Printing Office, 2001), 14–15.

13. Randall Kennedy. *Race, Crime and the Law* (New York: Vintage Books, 1998), 151, 153.

14. American Civil Liberties Union. *Driving While Black* (New York: American Civil Liberties Union, 1999).

15. Ball State University, "National Media Survey," Muncie, IN, 2003. This survey was conducted in the fourth quarter of 2002 among all 1,421 operating, non-satellite television stations, and a random sample of 1,490 radio stations.

16. Donald Bogle. *Toms, Coons, Mulattoes, Mammies, and Bucks: An Interpretive History of Blacks in American Films*, 3rd ed. (New York: Continuum, 2002), 433.

Index

About the Author

DENNIS ROME is Professor of Criminal Justice at the University of Wisconsin at Parkside. He is a Carnegie National Scholar and recipient of a Fulbright Scholarship.